TRIGGERS ARE THE GUIDES, Part I

TRIGGERS ARE THE GUIDES, Part I

Coming of age as a spiritual medium

M. LOVE

Triggers are the Guides, Part I text Copyright© 2021 by M. Love.

All rights reserved. No part of this book may be reproduced in any form or by any electronic or mechanical means including information storage and retrieval systems, without permission in writing to the author. The only exception is by the editor, Marie Valentine, who may quote short excerpts in a review.

Cover designed by Shaina "Toushai" Negron.

Disclaimer: This book is a work of creative nonfiction. The events are portrayed to be to the best of M. Love's memory. Names have been changed to protect the privacy of people involved. Many parts of this book, however, have fictional parts in varying degrees, for different purposes including literary effect. The conversations in the book come from recollections of the author's experiences and are not representations of word-for-word transcripts.

M. Love
Visit my website at www.mloveauthor.com

Printed in the United States of America. Independently Published Book.

First Printing: March 2021

Kindle Direct Publishing ISBN- 9798596271447

Dedication

I dedicate this book to those who feel, see, hear, taste, and smell. This book is especially for those who push through each door they are faced with, no matter what's on the other side.

Table of Contents

Dedication .... *v*
Foreword: Chance and Change .... *vii*
Let us Start from the Top *1*
Acceptance of Everybody is Important *7*
Kenneth's Early Life *11*
The Move to Forestbrook Drive *17*
What Happened to Father *23*
Continuation Through the First Decade *29*
Elementary Years, Setting Foundation, and Grounding *47*
Family and Friends: Second Grade *71*
Visiting Pop *83*
Third Grade *93*
Negative Energies *105*
A Reckoning *115*
Family Therapy *123*
Elma's Illness *137*
Rolling with the Punches *149*
Life After Elma's Peaceful Exit *167*
September 2001 .... *175*
Antics with Chad's Company *183*
Intermediate School *197*
The Return to our Hometown *249*
Fast Track into the Eighth Grade *261*
The Eighth Grade *283*
Epilogue *299*
Acknowledgements *301*
Summary of the Clairs *303*
References *306*

Foreword: Chance and Change

Pain changes people ... but pain has changed me in a positive way. It allowed me to feel the difference between what I had control of and what I could only sit back and watch, helplessly. Pain feels like watching your home burning before your eyes: It is so painful, but there is nothing further. The only thought going through one's head in this position of pain is to strategize the near future. What are the proceeding steps one will take?

Pain is the gift and curse within itself. Planning accordingly and being prepared for what is to surface in time is the best thing I did. However, the adversity and pain will cause one to go through change. Whether these changes are positive or negative, they will result from the circumstances of pain.

Life can be described in many words, but there is not an individual word that can fulfill the meaning of life. Many people claim that life is an experience and that it has its difficulties. Life is a gift and a curse given to us the moment our parents conceive, as well as the moment that we were fated to return to Earth for more tasks to complete. Being brought into life in this world is an ambiguous event not understood by humans, regardless of science, modern technology, and intelligence. We must not forget that our lives are all that we know, for it is the universal proof of our existence. Be reminded, however, that our souls will carry on after our existence in the physical world we call life.

In my life, I have met many who have contributed in various ways to the individual that I am today, in ways that were positive, negative, or neutral. Only a few, however, have made such an impact on my life that I could not be more grateful to have crossed paths with them. It is safe to say that those who have forcibly rewired the way that I perceived and reacted to life have made an impact for which I am thankful to have received.

In my twenty-something years of age, I am on the outside now, looking in. I am a molecular biologist working as a cell & gene therapy scientist by profession, and a born psychic medium outside of my professional career. My life in science came about in my adulthood, but my life in the spiritual world has been incorporated in my life for as long as I can remember. A controversy exists in the work that I do around the clock in both fields, and people who discover that I live my life through two realms of work that are categorically "opposite" often question me. Many people question my beliefs, experiences, professions, understanding and teachings, and they wonder how my life feels balanced as both a scientist and a psychic medium. There is a lot of relativity in between the metaphysical (spiritual) and physical (gross) world, and many thought-provoking events that I have endured confirm that somehow, someway, everything is one. In all, my experiences are one of many reasons for writing this book to introduce my light on these two realms through the eyes of myself. The big questions are why and how I am the way that I am.

I would like to reinforce that the title of this book, *Triggers Are the Guides*, explains how triggers will help you, the reader, evolve and live your life. My goal is, always, to help others succeed in the balancing of their physical, emotional, spiritual, and mental senses. In doing so, I see the immense emotion beyond what I have experienced, and I see how ugly some people truly can appear on the outside. I have removed myself from situations that were hurtful and people who were ill in their own misery. I realized the importance of connecting through the physical world and going into the spiritual to connect and regather myself.

I have my spiritual journey to thank for my ability to persevere through the physical world of life thus far. One would think that life would be difficult and lonely without much family to turn to for advice, but it is in fact the opposite. Although you will note in this book that I was living in my household, I was apart from my family at one point, which will be revealed in the second manuscript, Triggers are the Guides Part II. Without my physical family to lean on for the support I needed as a growing child, I received much guidance from my higher spirit, my spirit guides, loved ones who have passed on, and others who have helped along the way. They have guided my soul and young heart to where I am sitting today. Without their love and direct fostering of my mind, body, and soul, I cannot imagine where life would have taken me.

In addition, I have learned to acknowledge that my spirit guides have led me to the path that I am on, and I cannot thank them enough. This book about Carla is based on true stories … and through the stories I share, I will exemplify that not everything one is going through deems itself as the "end" or a permanent failure. It is an honor to write this book, as this book you are about to dive into looks at the legacies of many lives lived within my soul and others'.

We are one higher being that we cannot touch with our fingertips or feel with our toes, but we can feel in our energy that we are united. Because we are one, I consider the book a legacy to every life lived on Earth, because we can relate to one another through the gift of language as well as spirit and being human. Let us come in tune with one another and let me enlighten you with the power of my world combining with yours. On each page, we will be in unison.

"The start is today. The triggers are the guides." This quote was on a social media post that I saw, and the phrase deeply resonated with me. Unfortunately, the author was deemed unknown. However, if you are the author of the quote and find this, I would like to thank you for posting that powerful phrase in my sight. Truly, the title of this book holds true to this life path. My guides are made of many bodies, which includes my loved ones who have passed on to the other side, my transient spirit guides, and the Mother Earth that I walk upon and live in every waking day. Today is my day to start sharing my life in creative nonfiction with you.

As a woman in my twenties, I have a lot to offer to the world in terms of wisdom and a different perspective in my thought process. Let us start by talking about today: presently April 30, 2017. Today

FOREWARD: CHANCE AND CHANGE

I woke up, knowing that it is the day that my father had passed away twenty years ago by suicide. Today, I had to travel to south New Jersey to visit his grave and pay my respects, but I woke up with a satisfying feeling of inner peace. Inner peace is an emotion that I strive deeply to achieve in all aspects of life, and that is where my state of mind was this morning. The inner peace is because my father is one of my guides, and even though he is always with me in spirit, I wanted to be where we laid him to rest at the cemetery. It was my day to give him a huge thank-you for being one of my spirit guides for twenty years. My twin sister, Anne, my friend Marie, and I took the trip to south New Jersey to see his grave. As always, it was such a peaceful and harmonious time to be with these two. On our way down the Garden State Parkway, we were singing songs by Cher, Michael Jackson, Mariah Carey, and other artists from the 1980s and 1990s. Marie and I as always were yelling at Anne, because she has a tendency of changing the song at the best parts! Anne loved to change the song as we tried to belt out the high octaves of Mariah Carey or Christina Aguilera and laugh at how bad we sounded. Between the music during the car ride and people-watching the other drivers, there was so much laughter. We repeatedly lowered the music because we started to reminisce and giggle about stories during our seven years of friendship with Marie.

My twin and I saw many symbols that day that clearly showed us that Father knew that we were going to visit his grave. Throughout the drive, we'd spotted several hawks flying above the car, along with a cardinal in front of my home that morning. Hawks symbolize a spirit guide's presence and are a sign of divine protection. On the other hand, cardinals symbolize the presence of a loved one who has passed. In town, we saw a truck with the word "Mayflower" on the side, which is the boat that we believe transported his ancestors to the United States from Europe. You will learn more about my father within the book, but in the present day, he is one of my many spirit guides and guardians during my time here in gross spirit, thanking my father and others repeatedly.

Without further ado, welcome to ... *Triggers Are the Guides*.

Let us Start from the Top

This is where it all started—well, maybe. I wish I could go back further than what you are about to read, but this should suffice. I want to start by giving some background of my parents' lives, mostly my mother, before I existed in gross spirit on this Earth, to provide a better understanding of the mindset of her life transitioning into mine. Ready, set, go.

My mother was born into the gross world in the mid-twentieth century as a woman of Sicilian descent named Viola Trotta. Her father, George, was from Palermo, and her mother, Giovanna, was from Italy. Viola was born shortly before her parents' separation, when her father left for Florida to start a new life. Based on what I have gathered, the separation between my grandparents seemed to be going okay until a few months passed. After a few months of being separated, George kidnapped his young daughter Viola, and brought her to Florida to stay with him. At that time, locating a missing person using technology and methods of law enforcement was much different from the twenty-first century. There were no cell phones available to the public, no GPS tracking, no social media networks, nor were there more rapid means of getting a lead on the whereabouts of Viola. It was frightening for my grandmother, Giovanna, to try to locate my mother, but she had a good inkling that her ex-husband kidnapped Viola. Giovanna was able to retrieve Viola from George after a few weeks, but only because he dropped her off while no police officers were monitoring my grandmother's house. There was no trace of evidence to do anything to George such as get him arrested, but his kidnappings occurred a few times after the initial incident. George was sneaky and methodical, and clearly did not want to fully separate from his wife or his newborn daughter. When Viola was less than five years old, he disappeared out of thin air and my grandmother or Viola never heard from him again.

For most of my childhood, Viola was in search of her father, who she discovered was lost in the Witness Protection Program. There was no proof of his existence even though my mother had his Social Security card, a bank account statement, and a birth certificate. As you will read in the book, my mother finally told me that she was searching for him for years, and she was obsessed. At least we know the Witness Protection Program works, since she could not locate him, but there were little snippets that my mother had such as newspaper articles from the kidnappings and other legal issues to prove his existence.

I am sure that my grandfather is deceased at this point, and I have never attempted to connect with him through mediumship. I recall many instances growing up of seeing a car sitting on the corner of our street, such as a black Lincoln Town Car with tinted windows and two men sitting inside. I would also hear my mother receive unusual phone calls in the middle of the night, and the conversation was always in Italian. There was usually a worried tone in my mother's voice when the phone calls occurred, especially when she would tell the unknown man on the phone "Not to take care of him" or "Don't worry about it, I do not need you to do anything to him."

Through searching for many years, my mother finally located her father's whereabouts recently, as well as the other children and wives George had. I met two aunts and one uncle from George's side of the family in the beginning of the twenty-first century. With my mother's obsessive effort to search for him, she was able to learn that her father George passed years prior and was deemed a John Doe until the private investigation commenced for his whereabouts.

My mother was the oldest of five girls, the other four were born from her stepfather. According to her, she always felt like the outcast of her siblings. It was not until her eighteenth birthday, when she went to the town to obtain her birth certificate and other identification documents, that she learned that she was the daughter of George. According to her mother, she recalled the memories of being kidnapped before the age of five, and she believed that these memories were lucid dreams as a child, but it was on her eighteenth birthday that she learned the truth from her mother, who explained to her that the memories were real. My grandmother then proceeded to tell her that she was indeed the only child that she had with George, but my grandmother would not provide details on how to find him. Viola likely knew this at the time, but she felt that there was always the possibility that she had other siblings outside of her four siblings.

My maternal grandfather Michael, who I knew growing up, was the father of my four maternal aunts, and he seemed like a wonderful man to me. I will be sure to mention him again later, but it is worth noting that he seemed like a fair man who was straightforward and open to anyone and everyone. He would not tolerate bullshit, but he enjoyed having fun.

Fast-forward several years into the late 1970s. My mother received master's degrees in chemistry and mathematics, and a teaching license. I do not remember her work experience fully, but I do remember that I saw her resume once, and it was lengthy with experience in the mathematical field. At the beginning of her career, she started teaching in a high school in northern New Jersey. She taught her first class at around twenty-three years old.

Around this time, Viola was dating a man named James who unfortunately got into a car accident soon after and died on the scene. My mother told me that the steering wheel went through his chest, and he went straight to heaven. Shortly after James passed, Viola started dating his brother Kenneth. Kenneth and my mother got married a few years later in California. I would like to note here that I have connected with my Uncle James through a mediumship reading, and he identifies as one of my spirit guides. Typically, a spirit guide is defined as a guide for one's experience here in the gross realm and has walked the Earth before you arrived. James loved my mother so much, according to the mediumship reading I received once, and now watches over me.

Kenneth and Viola conceived my older brother and sister a few years after their marriage. Chris is my older brother, and he is seven years older than me. My older sister's name is Giovanna, from her grandmother, and she is two years older than me. Around the time that my older sister was born, Kenneth and Viola were already starting to have issues in their marriage. My father was drinking a lot at bars because he was unhappy, and my mother wanted him home, as any married woman would. I do not know the details, but it was my understanding from my mother that things between them were toxic and unmatched in terms of communication, senses of responsibility, and basic philosophies of life. According to Viola, Kenneth was mentally abusive and almost cheated on her on their wedding night.

In time, when their marriage was not improving, Viola had an affair with one of her first students that she met in her first year of teaching, Chris. As a result, Viola became pregnant. Although I am unsure if Viola knew that she was pregnant with Chris's child, my twin and I were successfully born in the early 1990s.

According to my mother, my twin Anne was supposed to be the first baby based on her positioning throughout the pregnancy via proof of sonograms. Before Viola gave birth to us, I shifted toward the "exit only" orifice, the exit strategy for all children, and I became Baby A. During my mother's birthing of us, I was born naturally, but my twin was born via caesarean section. Anne was born two minutes after me. She entered this world grey in color due to an umbilical cord wrapped around her neck. It still amazes me that two minutes went by and delivery doctors retrieved her safely and securely. We were healthy and content, and ready to start this round of life reincarnated together again. My twin and I have clearly been together through several incarnated lives. As you will see, it would have been unfathomable for us to come here this time around as one person. My father Kenneth documented himself as our father on both birth certificates, which leads to my inclination that my mother was not aware we were not his children.

A few weeks after we were born, a letter came in the mail addressed to my mother from the hospital where we were born. This letter detailed that blood results from my twin and I came back to be heterozygous (since every gene is comprised of two alleles, having one dominant allele and one recessive allele is heterozygous) in having the sickle hemoglobin gene, which meant that I was a carrier for sickle cell disease. Since this letter detailed that I have what's defined as the sickle cell trait, this would not have been possible if Viola and Kenneth were my parents. To be forthright, sickle cell disease is found in people of African and Jewish descent, and the gene to make someone a carrier is passed along from someone that is of this descent. Or a relative of this descent. Chris, Viola's friend, is African American, and Kenneth, her husband, is of European descent. On the day that the letter arrived, Kenneth realized that my twin and I were not his biological children. I am not sure who picked up the piece of mail that day, but that discovery did not go so well. The story continues.

Acceptance of Everybody is Important

Now, one may think at this moment Kenneth chose to leave my mother Viola and end their marriage for good. Instead, he reached out to Chris, my biological dad, and told him that he would never see his children again. My father made it clear to my mother that he intended to raise us without Chris's presence or input. This was good news for my mother, since Kenneth decided to stay with her, and she took advantage of the fact that Kenneth swallowed his pride to accept my twin and me as his children. Kenneth's forgiveness through accepting us as his children was not enough to show Viola that she needed to work hard to keep their marriage afloat as well.

In my opinion, this event was her chance to prove that she was grateful for my father's forgiveness, and to put in more effort to be a wonderful wife to him. In being a wonderful wife, I define this as seeking counseling for the two of them to work through the recent changes in the household as well as any residual trauma which Kenneth or Viola carried within them. Kenneth has a twin sister whom I recently reconnected with, and she informed me that my mother used to speak poorly to Kenneth and constantly treat him with disrespect. It was my understanding from Maria, my father's twin, that my mother would say verbally abusive things like, "Go talk to your family, and let them save you." To me, this indicates that my mother knew something was mentally off in my father's outlook on life and thus spirit. Instead of working within her marriage to solemnly work through his mind and soul for the peace he yearned, she suggested he get help from his parents and siblings.

At four years old, we traveled to southern New Jersey to see my father's parents on several occasions. His parents completely ignored my twin and me when we said hello to them, which in hindsight I can understand. I have always been polite, and I say hello to someone when I lock eyes with him or her. Kenneth's parents consistently ignored us at each visit, and I recall every moment in which they looked me square in the eye while doing so. I was an innocent four-year-old girl, what could be so harmful about me? I remember his parents making a comment to my mother, "Do not bring those negro babies to my house, because they aren't blood." They made many similar remarks such as this. I remember my mother arguing with her in-laws because she knew that Kenneth accepted us in the safety of our house, but Kenneth would not defend us in front of his parents when we visited. I remember how tense the energy was the last time I saw his parents, at four years of age, and I did not care to see them again, because they did not approve of the color of our skin. It was one thing to be upset with my mother for birthing two babies who are not their son Kenneth's, but it was another thing to make comments about our skin color, especially since at that age, Anne and I could comprehend their comments. There will always be two sides to every story, no matter how intense or trivial the situation is, but I will never forget the energy that situation left in my soul. I felt pure rejection from my "grandparents." At four years old, I did not feel like their grandchild because to them, I am just a negro child.

Nevertheless, my father Kenneth was mentally in a rough place. Throughout the years of attempting to grasp why Kenneth was in a dark state of mind, I learned from many people that he had undergone a phenomenon that I like to compare to the Multiple Hit Theory in cancer biology. This term was first proposed in 1953 pertaining to the hypothesis that cancer is a result of multiple hits of accumulated mutations to one's DNA in a cell (it can be many mutations happening at the same time in different ways). The Multiple Hit Theory causes detrimental effects in the cell's DNA downstream, and when these cells are going through cellular division and creating replicates in a semiconservative manner, there is no turning back for things to get out of control. In understanding what led him to his death, ruled suicide by asphyxiation, I realized only a few years ago that he was a humanized result of the Multiple Hit Theory. Here is the life of Kenneth, in which he exemplified the Multiple Hit Theory in human form, before I entered his world.

Kenneth's Early Life

I would like to point out that everything is from hearsay, and I never spiritually channeled with Kenneth to retrieve the information or explanation. I do not feel it is appropriate to channel him for the purpose of inquiring about sensitive information such as the reasons for his death, because bringing the energy connection to a reflective yet dark place may not be ideal for me.

In his immediate family, there were four children, including my father. The first two children born were boys (Michael and James), and Kenneth's parents wanted a girl next. When Kenneth's mother became pregnant, she discovered that she was having twins. She hoped for two twin girls, which would perfectly complement the two boys she already had. To her disappointment, she was having a boy and a girl. In the mid-twentieth century, she gave birth to both Kenneth and Maria, her last children. Kenneth's mother resented that she birthed him, her third son, and not two twin girls. According to my mother, Kenneth's mother used to dress him in girly clothes such as dresses and skirts, and she'd ask him to do girly things in her presence to make her feel like she had two daughters. Kenneth's parents treated him differently, and his existence was clearly unwelcomed from them. Kenneth was the outcast, yet his parents adored Maria, showering her with joy, since she was the little girl and they always wanted her.

Kenneth and Maria were very close, and that was unchanged given the way his parents treated him. Overall, Kenneth felt like he was second in line after his twin sister. I am sure he never questioned his parents' displacement of love, but trying to figure out his displacement in life almost did not matter in comparison to the pain and thus change of his existence. This was Multiple Hit #1 of three hits.

Multiple Hit #2 started when his older brother James passed away. My mother was dating James at the time he passed away, and it was only a matter of time before my mother started dating my father. Although my mother married Kenneth after dating his older brother James, the last hit was when she cheated on him and got pregnant with my twin and me. Of course, I am thankful to be on this Earth, as I have a lot of work to do spiritually and scientifically to project forward to others. However, my mother's actions and handling of the marriage were the final hit, Multiple Hit #3. I am sure that there were so many instances in between the three hits, but these are the hits of which I am aware. The third hit was a gift and curse, in that we are two children meant to be here by the grace of God.

I remember a lot from the first few years of my life when I had Kenneth as my father. I know what he liked, what he did not like, the things he used to do for the family and for my twin and me, and I remember his mood swings. He used to like Marlboro Red cigarettes, Yosemite Sam, and cooking. He was a Le Cordon Bleu specialty chef and a firefighter. He loved corned beef sandwiches with mustard, and he made sure to prepare a sandwich with his homemade batch of corned beef every morning. As he got into his car every morning, he would stick his sandwich out the window and let my twin and I have a quick bite before he drove off. To this day, corned beef reminds me of him and makes me think of what else made him happy. He would wake up early during the weekend and cook breakfast for everyone in his boxers and blue-ribbon chef's hat. One year, for my older sister's birthday, Father baked her a cake from scratch and literally carved a small edible statue of Ariel from The Little Mermaid to sit beautifully on top of the cake. His carving was flawless, as he decorated the cake with seashells and other beautiful trinkets in a professional presentation. I have seen many pictures of him in culinary school, and he was able to make art out anything. For instance, he carved the Statue of Liberty with butter using his bare hands. It was amazing to see how talented he was at cooking, and I thought it was magical when I was a kid.

Other than that, the last few memories that I had of him were not so great. Most people do not recall memories as young as four or five, but my memory serves me from an early age. Father had tendencies to drink obsessively and stumble into the house in the wee hours of the night. When the confrontations started to get worse between my father and my mother, it was because he came home drunk to start an argument. From my recollection, during these confrontations she used to sit in silence and let him continue to spatter disrespectful things to her. I have no doubt that my mother deserved it at times, because she has always had a tendency of not thinking before she speaks and can be very hurtful. He never laid a hand on her, but he used to get extremely close to her face and be verbally abusive until she shut down.

On many occasions, my older brother Chris would try to jump in, since he was the oldest and technically next in line to be the man of the house. When my brother attempted to intervene, father always took his focus off my mother and lashed out on him. As clear as day, I remembered my father grabbing my brother's dark green shirt and completely ripping it off him. It was clear that his drunk anger made him completely lose his mind and control over his actions.

My father felt powerless in his mind, and even at my young age, I noticed that. Father felt the separation from my mother and her verbally abusive ways, and thus he occupied himself with alcohol as his outlet. Alcoholism, as many know and suffer from in their family lineage, truly separated the spirit I saw in the mornings and other times that he was happily existing. Anyway, my father felt the tension from Chris because he was defending his mother, and he felt everything spiraling in front of him. As the familial energy in the house worsened between my father and mother, my mother decided to allow her best friend Elma to move into the house with the family.

Elma and my mother met in the town where my mother worked in northern New Jersey. They accompanied each other as they smoked marijuana and surely other drugs together all the time. Elma and Mother were best friends for quite some time, minimally one decade, before the four of us kids existed. Their friendship was one of her first in her career, from what Mother has explained to me in my earlier years. I was around five when I met Elma as she moved into our house. Within a week or so of Elma moving in, we were packing to move out of the house to the other side of town.

As we were working towards the big move across town, we did not see our father as much, because he continued to spend his evenings out of the house and drinking excessively. In my hometown we refer to neighborhoods based on the elementary school located nearby: West End, East End, and Stony Brook. When it was time to move out of the West End house, everyone packed their bags and made their way across town to the East End.

The Move to Forestbrook Drive

The house that we moved into was on a street called Forestbrook Drive. Let us state the obvious here: the street sounds like a haunted house, right? Now, one may think I am joking, but I am not exaggerating that this was the name of the street. I do not have the exact date on which we moved in, but I am sure that there would be some spiritual symbolism behind it. Maybe a numerology interpretation could have added to the spookiness of the location and the dynamic energy setting for that moving day.

For those that do not know numerology, it is defined as the predictions set forth by the power of numbers or the vibrations of the numbers, related to the event, the day, the time frame, the birthdate and time, or name of the person. Numerology is one of many aspects that proves how the energy of the world and person is relative to the numbers in their birth, and it is scarily accurate. There are aspects related to the date and birth name an individual is born with such as life path number, soul number, karmic numbers, destiny numbers, outer personality number, inner personality number, and so on. Numerology is widely accepted by folks who do not understand "heavier" spiritual practices that are metaphysical, such as reiki, psychic mediumship, or clairvoyant healings.

Although we do not know the exact date that we moved into the house, based on the files I located, my parents purchased the Forestbrook Drive home in 1997 for $132,000 (the numerology number for the purchase price is $1 + 3 + 2 = 6$). The number six in numerology symbolizes the mark of the beast, for which the common example is the number 666. The mark of the beast is not necessarily negative or dark-spirited because from a different perspective, in the phrase "mark of the beast," the beast could be a mindset, a choice, or something more positive to channel the energy into huge changes. The number six further represents the power of protection, sacrifice, domestic partnership, and choices. The numerological vibration of the house purchase year is the number eight ($1 + 9 + 9 + 7 = 26$, or 8); eight also happens to be my destiny and karma number. Destiny and karma numbers are related to fate and "what goes around comes back around," respectively. For this, my fate in the language of numerology exemplifies that I need to fulfill and reclaim my personal power to what depowers me through the vibration of eight. It is a conundrum that my destiny and karma number is eight as well as the purchase year.

The day we moved in truly set the tone for our new home welcoming to the East End of town at Forestbrook Drive. My mother drove us children to the house initially before we started moving the belongings in. We entered the house together, and my mother was annoyed to see that there was furniture leftover in the living room and dining room. One peculiar piece of furniture was a small table in the living room area, with a note that the previous owner left for my mother. The note said something to the gist of the following:

Viola,

My apologies. I could not hold this from you, as this has become very important for me to tell you why I moved out of this house. This house is not safe or sacred for my wrongdoings. It did not turn out as I intended. There were rituals that I performed here. It was too much for me, and this house is now yours. You will not find me after this, but I must say that I am sorry. Good luck.

-Geraldine

As one could see, this letter was a warning to my mother about the energy of the house. Her warning, simply put, said that she did some rituals, could not control the energy of this house anymore, and good luck to us. How could someone do this to a family of four children? When the others and I read the letter over my mother's shoulder, she took the paper and quickly put it in her pocket. Nevertheless, it was too late. We'd read the letter. Chris was staring at her because he could not believe what he thought he read. Nevertheless, at this point, it was too late to turn back on the house. We already left the West End house, and my mother already purchased this house. There was no turning back.

For the remainder of that day, the move-in was quiet and obdurate, as we watched our mother laughing to herself because she could not fathom what she just read on the peculiar table left behind. As I watched her move bags and boxes, cursing under her breath and slowly losing her shit, I felt a sense of foreboding coming along. She was terribly annoyed, in a panic because she felt helpless. Geraldine and my mother had connected during the house closing, and my mother visited her quite frequently before the actual move. I met her once. She was a frail Caucasian woman with curly red hair, and she was a little aggressive looking. My mother did try to contact Geraldine on that moving day and was expectedly unsuccessful.

As I observed my mother throughout the move, it was as if she already had absorbed some of the negative energy. It was as though she was connecting inadvertently with the spirits in the surrounding perimeter of the house.

For those unaware of the basic rules of spirits and energy, they travel in the same fashion that particles do. For instance, when someone farts and it travels across the room or when someone is blowing smoke from their lungs after taking a pull of a cigarette, the particles will travel due to the law of diffusion, and the presence could be sensed. In those moments as I watched my mother unpack into our new home, I could sense the spirit and energy in my third eye leaking through her energy field, or aura, by harboring around. To circle back to the numerology symbolism of the number six, the mark of the beast stands on the thin line in its perspective of negative or positive for the purchase of this home.

Regarding the third eye, I have added a small *Reference* section at the end of this book to encompass the definition of the third eye (known as one of the Clairs), the Multiple Hit Theory, and other things that are mentioned throughout. I encourage you, the reader, to head back there to learn a smidge of science, spirituality, and other things. Learning is truly a progression through life's journey, and it never ends. One of the many keys to happiness is to be a student of life as well as being openminded to learning material and different perspectives. Now, back to the story as to where things left off after the move from the West End to Forestbrook Drive.

What Happened to Father

As mentioned previously, Elma moved in with us and after the move into Forestbrook Drive, it was evident that my parents were on bad marriage terms. A few weeks went by and my parents were arguing so aggressively we could hear them while we were playing outside in the driveway or yard. The Forestbrook Drive area was in the shape of a U, and my street was the bottom end of the U-shaped streets. There is a map in the back of this book to reference this street and the nearby areas where the genesis of this story takes place.

One day, shortly after we moved in, Giovanna, my twin Anne, and I were outside playing basketball in the driveway. Anne loves basketball, and my mom generously purchased a basketball hoop to place in the driveway to practice her skills. I was not into basketball at the time, but I enjoyed playing with my forever-best friend Anne in the driveway to accompany her. While we were there shooting hoops, my father walked outside and suddenly Giovanna stopped dribbling. We all stared at Father, with Giovanna nearest him; Anne staggered behind her, followed by me. He was clearly sobbing and seemed extremely hurt and defeated. He walked up to his Giovanna and hugged her tightly. He walked up to my twin first, then me, and hugged us. He did not say a word to us, not a *Goodbye* or a *See you later* as he walked to his car to leave. We did not see him for a few days, possibly weeks.

We saw him again on the day my older sister Giovanna was receiving her First Communion from the Catholic Church in our town in April. While we were at the church during the ceremony, Father was not at the church, and we did not expect him to come. We celebrated afterward at our new house. Everyone in the family showed up, including my mother's side of the family and my father's side, excluding him. During the celebration, Giovanna was prancing around the yard. Then, Father made the effort to show up to see Giovanna and extend his congratulations. All I could remember was walking down the driveway to see him arriving in his white station wagon. He opened the car door, smiling, and made his way to Giovanna to greet her. He smiled at my sister and me, but he did not look at anyone else or attempt to have a conversation with any family members, including my mother. After he congratulated Giovanna for receiving Communion, he walked toward his car and looked back to her one last time. He got in the car and drove away, and barely anyone noticed his presence, but I saw the entire thing. The celebration for Giovanna's Communion continued, and no one questioned his brief presence that day.

A few days went by, and Kenneth had not returned home since his transient visit to see Giovanna at her Communion party. Truthfully, even at five years old, I thought about how long it had been since he had been home. I did not believe that my mother had a rational reason to kick him out or leave him, but there are unknowns. He was our father, and in my observations at the time, he had not done anything severe enough to have the separation be real. Maybe it was Mother's wrongdoings or failure to formally divorce or amend the marriage that caused his immense absence. Several days after the Communion, my mother went ahead and filed a missing person's report in town.

On the last night of April, a spiritual presence woke me up, urging me to awaken from my sleep. This was not the first time a spirit had awoken me, so I did not seem scared or surprised. I do not recall the first encounter of a spiritual presence waking me up, but it was not a shock to me to be pressed to be awoken. Either way, I understood through claircognizance that the spirit insisted I get out of my bed. At five years of age, walking down the hallway, I made my way to my brother Chris's bedroom. Chris was snoring, per usual, and I climbed around him on the bed to look out of his bedroom window. I opened the window, and there he was. Kenneth. Kenneth was in the backyard, just below the window I was looking out, and he was cutting our garden hose, still attached to the water line on the house, with a chisel saw. I looked down to him, and he looked up at me and angrily whispered, "Carla, get back inside and close the window. Now!"

As any five-year-old girl would do when they are caught spying on a parent, I panicked and closed the window. I did not understand why he was in the backyard, and why he was not inside the house sleeping with my mom. I could not comprehend why he was cutting our garden hose with a chisel saw. I raced back to my bedroom, in fear that he would come in the house and yell at me some more. In fear of his anger, I placed my blanket over my head and shut my eyes.

The morning came, and the memory of the previous night had already left me. I walked to school with my twin and Elma and continued with my day. As a few days passed, there was no news on my father's whereabouts or if he would ever come back home to us.

On the third day of May, police officers showed up to our house in search of my mother. Upon their arrival, police officers took their hats off and expressed that they'd located her husband Kenneth in the back of a nearby diner, a few towns over, expired from asphyxiation. They found him a few days after he had passed with the garden hose that I saw him cut the other night in the backyard. Police explained to Mother that one end of the garden hose was located on the exhaust pipe of his station wagon, and the other end inserted through the bottom of the car into the interior. It was bizarre to me that there was not much emotion irradiating from my mother, as it did not seem like much news to her. It struck me as her mental illness and insecurities intensified upon the news of her husband passing, and she laughed in disbelief. I cannot recall where Elma was, she might have traveled north to see her sister and son in that timeframe. The police brought to the house multiple suicide notes: one for Mother, one for us four children.

My father came to visit me in spirit the evening the police notified the family of his death. I was sleeping after a long night of tears and sobbing, and suddenly, I awoke from my sleep and I sat up to see Kenneth. Kenneth looked very calm yet sad, and he looked at me from the doorway of my bedroom. I saw him in white light, and he looked disappointed and ashamed to connect with me in this state. Although I did not understand what suicide meant at five years old, I understood his deeply saddened energy to see me in his other spiritual state and say goodbye to me.

He said, *"Hi Carla. I am sorry,"* and he sat there in silence while I looked on. I started to feel his fear, too. He knew that my clairsentience was noticing his fear, and he quickly said, *"Goodbye Carla,"* and vanished. I just remember waking up in the morning in tears and telling my twin that I saw Father one last time.

It was a couple of days for all of us. Chris and Mother wept the most after losing Kenneth. The days flew by, and the only part of the entire process that I remember is going to the funeral and the burial. At the funeral, I remembered Mother laughing belligerently because she said that he did not look like himself and looked horrible. It was very uncomfortable to see my mother laughing at her husband in his casket laid to rest. In fact, it was slightly sickening to me. At that moment, I looked over at my twin because I could not believe she was laughing manically, and she looked unstable while doing so. His parents did not look in the direction of my twin and me as the funeral and burial commenced that day, but his twin sister was with Mother and all of us children in support of the loss of our known father. I remembered how strong Maria was, working through the day and processing what this day meant for her, because that day she had to bury her twin.

As our mother's eyes rolled around the room in laughter and disbelief, my twin and I walked to the coffin to pay respects for the first time. Although I had never attended a funeral before, I asked him to talk to us when he was ready to and to guide us through what was to come next. I felt so much pressure in my heart, knowing that so much was to come from this circumstance. The funeral service came and went, and it was time to bring him to his resting place at the nearby cemetery in south New Jersey.

We arrived at the cemetery in which Kenneth and his three siblings as well as his parents had designated plots. James was already laid to rest, waiting for his brother. We buried him. We cried. We prayed. In addition, we mourned, for years to come.

Continuation Through the First Decade

I grasped the severity of what happened to my father Kenneth right away. He was my father on that day and for a long time afterward, so the pain was of losing a parent. There was no coming back and bringing him back home, or a way for my mother and him to work out their relationship again. Although it was tragic to see my mother distraught and uncomfortably giddy during his funeral, I knew that it was time to push forward with our lives and continue.

One of many anomalous things in our home started with the series of occurrences pertaining to the dark side of the spiritual world intervening with all interactions in the household. Geraldine's note immediately started to ring true in our new house, beginning on the evening we arrived home from Kenneth's burial. During that early evening, my siblings, Mother, and I were walking into the front door of the house after arriving home from our long drive from the cemetery. Elma met us in the driveway since she did not go with us, and we walked into the house one after another.

We started to enter the foyer area, and seconds later, I felt a burning sensation from the top of my left shoulder to near my elbow. It felt as if something scratched me, and I immediately screamed in agony. Nothing was sticking out from the closet located on the left wall of the foyer area, but my claircognizance kicked in to indicate that something scratched me deeply. I looked down to my side. There were three vertical tears in the skin of my shoulder, all in parallel formation. The scratches were as if the Wolverine from X-Men clawed me with three of his sharp claws but not as deep as if it were the Wolverine. The vertical scratches were evidently deeper than an average human fingernail scratch. I was there, bleeding, and utterly confused but frightened. The energy quickly turned eerie and intense, and I clearly observed fear in every person's eyes, including my mother.

My clairvoyance immediately envisioned an immoral spirit, and I then saw the confirmatory image of the evil person in my third eye. I focused and saw that the image of his face was evidently smiling, as this image of him with a huge grin remained in my head. He was clearly gesturing to me that he enjoyed seeing me in pain. In that second, I realized that something ill-willed and not alive did this. What baffled me the most was that it was strong enough to do this to me physically! This sort of thing happens in movies, but I would not have known that at my young age. Pain was the change, and I knew that I was literally bleeding, and there was fear scattered in the room.

My mother then looked at me and exclaimed, "How the fuck did that happen?" as the others looked on.

My brother was confused, looked at me, and said, "I have no idea how that happened, and none of us touched or scratched her." I looked at Mother again to seek her guidance on this, since she knows best as my mother. She looked at me and told me to go clean myself up. In disappointment, I walked up the stairs into the bathroom and thought about how I was five years old, cleaning up my own cut. The confusion in this circumstance was a solid tie between the spirit that I saw in my third eye and the fear that came from within, as well as the lack of guidance that my mother delivered to the situation. Everyone was silent as I proceeded to the bathroom, wiped myself off with soapy water, and placed several bandages from the cupboard over the wounds. I finished wiping myself down and headed to my room in silence and tears of shock. My twin entered the room and stared at me in equal confusion, but she did not say anything. She did not have to say anything, because we understood one another in the moment. We knew that Mother must have been insensitive from losing her husband.

Upon waking up the next morning, I realized that something was different and powerfully negative in the house. It was after this day that everyone started to notice more spiritually intense things happening in the house. Mother started locking herself in her bedroom, and my twin and I took the initiative to investigate and discover how the remainder of the house told the story. We wanted to understand what may have happened in this home before we arrived and why the energy was so powerful. Around this time, it was probably a month or two after our father passed.

We started with the backyard. We observed several large trees and small areas that may have been burial areas. The height of the weeds and grass in the yard were evident that the lawn remained unattended for a long time. To finalize our backyard quest, we spotted a creek running at the end of our property. On the backside of the house, there was a dining-room door leading to the outside but with no stairs or porch attached to the exit. As days went by, we discovered that there was an attic, but no one could access it. We did have access to the basement and started to look through it. The first time Anne and I went into the basement, we immediately felt as though someone was staring at us from the corner of the room. The energy down there was dense, as if we were in a black space with no particulates in the room. There were two small basement windows to my recollection, but no cellar door. We noticed a secret passageway that seemed to start behind the washer/dryer setup.

My twin and I waited until we were able to sneak away downstairs on a random Saturday morning, and we walked in front of the washer machine to enter the secret passageway. We stared at one another in decision of who will go behind the washer machine. Then, we played a game of rock-paper-scissors to see whoever loses out of three. My twin lost the short game, but she persuaded me to go back there because she was petrified to go back there. I did not care to argue, since it was daytime, so I let it go and agreed with a flashlight in my hand.

My twin helped me up onto the platform at the washer and dryer setup, and I carefully stepped behind the dryer. I proceeded back to the passageway that clearly ran along the edges of the basement. This passageway was the outer perimeter of the basement, as if an animal used to run through there, as it seemed absent of footsteps. It was extremely dark back there, and there was about eight inches of space in diameter to squeeze myself through. The ground on which

I walked was unfinished and filled with uneven rubble. As I took a few steps, looking down to find my ground, I looked up to see a huge shadow in front of me. peering from around the corner. That shadow quickly shifted forward as if it were running from me, and before I could get around the next corner, I saw two sets of prisoner chains and shackles on the wall. Immediately, I turned around in pure fear to run back to the entranceway. My flashlight turned off as I accidently smashed it against the wall turning around and made my way back to my twin. I never went back in there again.

The following years were somewhat a blur and happened so fast, but so slow. Honestly, I knew that my father's death was only the beginning of our struggle as a family and household. My mother was in a different space in her mind. Her mindset turned unstable literally moments after receiving news of her husband passing by suicide. The suicide notes were in Mother's possession, in which I clearly recall his last words to her, *"You win,"* surely rang in her head. Now that there was the factored pressure of balancing the care of four children as well as herself physically, mentally, spiritually, and emotionally, we could be sure that living with her was not going to be smooth.

To reflect on the moment of my father's death, it was a circumstance that I fully comprehended and understood what could happen to life from Mother's viewpoint. I knew that he passed away; I knew that Mother did wrong by him, and they were separating before we saw him the last time. I did not know, however, why he was cutting the hose in the backyard that evening. I am grateful to have known that I was aware and able to wake up to go to my brother's window, to then open it up and see my father's face for the last time. I am sure that I am the last family member that saw our father, Kenneth, alive.

In the house, it was my mother, her friend Elma, and the four of us kids. Elma kept my mother company and spent a lot of time with her throughout the years. In the few years in which Elma was living under our roof, the mayhem began. The first thing that was noticeable was the shift in the energy when Elma came around. It was strange enough that Elma moved in not long before we relocated toward the East End of town. There was not much of an explanation for it, and there was no house meeting or conversation about her sudden appearance. Keep in mind, my father resided in the West End house, and at that time my parents were still together and "okay" in their marriage. It was not until we relocated to the East End of town when things turned sour between my parents. Regarding Elma, my initial impression was that she was staying with us to help us with the move, but I quickly observed that was not the case when she remained in the East End house after a few weeks. I remembered that she was leaving with Mother and slowly moving her belongings from her residence in northern New Jersey to our house. There was never an announcement about Elma residing in our new house on the East End of town.

For her daily routine, Mother used to wake up early around six a.m. to get ready for her workday and head out for her work in northern New Jersey, and Elma would wake us up around six thirty a.m. to prepare us kids for school. As my mom would get ready for work, Elma used to do our hair (us twins), whether it was in a braid or in a ponytail. It was a blessing in disguise that Elma helped us do our hair every morning, because I learned something every day about my curly hair and how many ways to style it. Elma also had curly hair like ours, but she styled it in a braid typically for simplicity. When my father was alive and we were living on the West End of town, Mother used to cut our hair down to a small afro. It was awful, especially since the kids at preschool used to make fun of us and tell us that we looked like little WOPs. If you are unaware what a WOP is, it stands for Without Papers. They used to make fun of my twin and I for not having long girly hair like the other girls. Additionally, since Mother spoke a lot of Italian to us at home, we were not aware that not every word was in the English language. Alongside the fact that we had afros and we were speaking part Italian and part English in pre-kindergarten; we were the youngest in our class. My mom was manipulative to the school in order to bypass the minimum age to get us into preschool early. We were at the cusp of the age range in which we should have started school the following year, but we would have then been slightly older than the other kids would. Since my mother was in the school systems by profession, she pushed very hard to ensure that we were in school as early as possible. Now that I look back, it was likely because she did not want to look at us any longer than she had to. Why do I say that? Because my twin and I were two unexpected bastard children who were born through infidelity and through a mistake that both of our parents made to create us. We lived through her pregnancy without termination. We were not Kenneth's children, but he did not turn us away.

Elma walked with my twin and me to school when we first moved to this part of town; we went to a school called Stony Brook Elementary for the last month or so of kindergarten. In this school, we made more friends in the short time we attended. With being a new student in the spring at Stony Brook, it was as if I blinked and kindergarten graduation was upon us. My twin and I met a friend named Jayden at Stony Brook, and he had a different looking hairstyle that anyone I have met: a Caesar cut with a triangle-shaped afro in the front of his head. He seemed silly like my twin and I, and ready to play with us during recess. Either way, it was cool to have someone acknowledge us, laugh with us, and introduce us to more kids in the school.

After kindergarten graduation, the instillment that we were without a father in our life remained a new wound, as we had to move forward as a family. My mother decided that my twin and I would start first grade in the elementary school on the East End of town. Elma gladly walked us to attend our first day. When my twin and I arrived to get in line to meet our classmates, I remembered one girl walked over to us immediately. She was smiling at us, and she said, "Oh hi, are you twins? My name is Caroline." I looked at her, smiled, and I said, "Yes, we are. This is my twin Anne, and my name's Carla." We instantly gained a friend, and she happened to have class with Anne. We stood in line, and Elma waved goodbye as we proceeded into the school building for class. Our first day at East End Elementary School was so refreshing, since all the kids were excited to meet one another and wanted to be there. We found out soon after that Caroline lived near our house, as she resided on one of the streets that created the U, Delacy Avenue. It was a nice start to our school year.

It was not long after we moved in that we met and discovered our neighbors, who were kids of all ages. My twin and I looked outside of the window one day and discovered several children playing in our quiet street, doing activities such as writing in chalk on the pavement to play hopscotch or running around the yards in the vicinity to play tag. There were two kids next door, and seven kids the next-door down. Across the street, three kids were around my old brother and sister's age, so that was convenient at the time. It was lovely when my twin and I went outside to introduce ourselves for the first time. They were readily eager to say hello and introduce us to their posse. From what I recall, the seven children that lived two doors down all were a year or two apart, ranging from ages three to about eleven at the time. It was so cool to me that all seven siblings of this family, the Nobels, were girls, predominately blonde-haired with blue eyes. My favorite two things about this family that I admired right away was that they attended home school—their mother taught them—and that they were all so centered in their spirit and positivity towards life already.

On the weekends, Elma woke up early with us in the morning to make breakfast before our day started. From the first day that she cooked us breakfast, I would shadow her to study how to cook myself breakfast one day. We used to have breakfast cooked for us during the weekend, but during the week, it was up to us kids to make ourselves cereal or oatmeal in the microwave. When Elma was finished with breakfast on Saturdays, she would leave the dishes in expectation that someone would do them. Then, she and Mother used to leave and run errands until late in the day. Elma and Mother used to spend the entire day together while us kids remained at home. After Elma and Mom arrived home, depending on their mood for the day, Elma prepared dinner. If not, we had to fend for ourselves. Usually, when Mother and/or Elma decided to cook, there was always an excess of food, usually pasta, saved as leftovers in a huge pot. She used to make a huge pot of sauce and leave the entire pot in the fridge for us to eat from, until it started to smell funny. Those leftovers would last us a week tops, and the next week was usually us figuring out what to salvage from the cabinets or refrigerator until she cooked again. That is how the food situation was in the household after Kenneth passed, mostly because he was not here to cook for us. Elma cooked for us here and there, but it decreased over time. Mother cooked very well, as she grew up in an Italian family that taught her how to cook meals and they ate together as a family every day.

On Sunday mornings, Mother used to bring us to the nearby Catholic Church, St. Joseph's, while Elma stayed home. Everyone except for Elma went to church until my twin and I received Communion when we were in the second grade. By this time, Mother stopped going to church, stopped cooking, and stopped cleaning. Elma may have expected that Mother was not contributing to doing much after my father took his life, because I never heard them argue about it. Clearly, Elma was a wonderful friend to her, or maybe there was something else there, such as an intimate relationship. We may never know, but looking back to my memories, it seems as though Elma was her lover. It did not matter to me because Elma was a mother figure to me, and I was secretly learning as much as I could from her to survive just in case she was not around anymore. I wanted to absorb and understand who and what Elma's purpose was in my life, but also learn to be independent from Mother's lack of care. It was clear that Mother was not contributing to my growth as a little human.

My mother's disappearances into her bedroom had not stopped since Kenneth's passing, and lasted days at a time as she dwelled with the door locked. She only came out to use the bathroom, since there was no bathroom attached to her bedroom. We used to call the bathroom the meeting room, because this was where we would see Mother and get to talk to her briefly before she quickly disappeared into her bedroom again. Noticeably, Mother's mission was to get in and out of the bathroom as fast as possible because she knew that we would bombard her with questions, updates, or things to discuss, or sometimes just for a small dose of affection. Mother looked so tired, as if she were half-asleep, and usually smelled funny when she used to come out of the bedroom. She was usually out of it. Now that I am older, I know that she was always high throughout my childhood. In understanding her choice of high, I was not completely sure at the time, but I will get into that as the story unfolds.

Mother worked in her profession, from my perspective, as if everything was okay at home, but she lingered in her depression when she came home. Although she enjoyed teaching chemistry and math, she was interested in biology and anatomy as well. When mother decorated the house at Forestbrook Drive, she brought home several jars containing pig fetuses, frogs, baby sharks, and other animals preserved in formaldehyde. The jars sat in the living room in replacement of home décor, and although this was before companies such as HomeGoods existed, it certainly was not typical décor for a living room. She had a microscope and a case of slides in the dining room area, but she never got around to teaching us how to use it and look at sample slides. Elma was not interested in any décor related to the beings in formaldehyde and did not care to teach us how to use the microscope. She focused on our wellbeing.

What interested me so much about Elma was that she had a son who was ten years older than I was and resided in northern New Jersey with her sister. Even still, Elma treated the four of us as if we were hers. Her son, Bobby, used to visit us on occasion during the weekend. Bobby got along with my brother Chris, and luckily, they were close in age. Chris and Bobby used to play basketball outside, play wall-ball, and do other fun things that teenage boys did. Either way, the relationship between Bobby and Elma seemed okay based on my observation, but it was unclear how the relationship truly stood. In every relationship with a family member or friend, I quickly learned that each person would have both positive and negative attributes.

The phrase "happy family" would not apply in terms of the dynamic at home amongst us siblings or household overall. It is unquestionably a normalcy to hear others tell stories about siblings fighting over toys, space, and time with parents (e.g., one child is favored more than the others are). However, the relationship between the four of us siblings was completely different due to the constant battle of my twin and me versus Giovanna and Chris. It was clear that Giovanna and Chris believed that we were not equal to them for many reasons. My twin and I were their younger siblings from infidelity, and it was their belief that we may have been the driving force for father's suicide. Giovanna and Chris were half-Italian and half Anglo-Saxon, and in many circumstances, the conversation always circled back to a gesture or remark about my twin and I being half African American. This was when Anne and I took a mental note that we may have a different father than them. In a group setting where friends or family members would come over, they always brought up the fact that their sisters were half-black so they could say the N-word or other phrases deemed inappropriate that black people apparently only say to fellow black people. Regularly, my siblings communicated to their black friends that they can relate to them better because their little twin sisters were also black. I often heard that conversation unfold in front of us as if we were too young to comprehend, or they did not care whether we heard. Elma did not tolerate any banter in her presence such as this, because she was also partially black.

With love in my heart toward Giovanna and Chris, I would not accuse my siblings of being racist, because they must have learned it from someone else. It may have been from their grandparents, their mother, or someone else. Since they were older than we were, their environment that influenced them is much different from mine. My twin and I noticed early on that their attitude toward us was not positively influential, as older siblings should be, but rather, at times, was more negative than normal. What is normal? Normal, in my definition, would be a little bickering here and there about minor issues, such as space to play in the house or hogging a video game. Yet, depending on their moods and the energy of the house, it influenced their behavior towards us.

An example of influential behavior change stemmed from times when Mother was in a gloomy mindset and loudly shouted in her bedroom statements like, "I cannot take it anymore, I cannot do this," or, "Someone please kill me, I don't want to be here anymore." Unfortunately, the energy exerted from her bedroom channeled into the negativity of my siblings, which then determined how they treated my twin and me. Elma came out to check on us more often than Mother because she was aware of the separation between us kids.

For starters, Giovanna had an attitude like a child who felt she deserved ice cream when she saw the ice-cream truck approaching. Giovanna had moments of acting civil with my twin and me, but each moment would last for seconds at a clip. She would then start yelling and walk away, sometimes telling us that we ruined everything for her. My brother, on the other hand, was undoubtedly strange in nature, and always seemed to have an eerie energy that was not right, which I did not understand at the time.

Truthfully, it was not long before the unexpected started happening and Chris's behavior came to the surface. It was the first time that I stayed home sick from school in the first grade, and Elma was not able to stay at home with me that day. She decided to hitch a ride with my mother to northern New Jersey to visit her family while my mom went to work. Mother asked Chris to stay home with me while I was still resting that morning, and I woke up around ten o'clock that morning, feeling okay. Usually, I missed school because I did not sleep well the night prior due to the strong spiritual energy pestering me through the night since moving into the Forestbrook Drive house. Ever since Anne and I explored the house to understand what Geraldine did to the house before we moved in, us siblings had all been waking up to unexpected disturbances through the night.

One night my twin and I woke up at the same time to see the closet door slide open and that grinning spirit that I saw in my third eye. When Anne described what she saw, with tears in her eyes, I knew that she saw the exact same spirit I did. We both did not tell anyone what happened that night, but Chris and Giovanna separately experienced similar things in the night in their rooms. At separate instances, I heard them going into each other's rooms explaining what woke them up a few moments prior in complete fear.

Another reason I would stay home from school was because I wanted to be with Elma and learn more of her wisdom on cooking, maintaining my hair since it was growing, cleaning, and whatever else I could extract from her motherly habits.

That morning when I decided to stay at home sick, I went downstairs and I noticed that my brother was there, but not Elma. Immediately, I thought it was strange, but I said hi and sat down next to him on the floor. I started watching cartoons with him, and after a few minutes of silence, I asked him where Elma was. He stated that Elma had to go to northern New Jersey and turned away to continue watching television. Sometime later, my brother told me that he was going to take a nap upstairs and that I should go with him so I was not alone downstairs. I nodded and followed him upstairs to his room. As we went to his room to lay down, I got into the bed with him, laying on my back, and closed my eyes. As I laid there, I opened my eyes again to see him facing me with his eyes closed. I thought to myself that I did not need to sleep, but I decided to lay there while he napped. On my back, I laid there in silence as I tried to fall asleep, but I knew that I would not be able to. It was not long before I noticed that my brother grabbed my pants and started taking them off. When I looked over, he had his eyes closed, as if he could not see what he was doing. In this moment, I stared at him in confusion, and he continued to undress me with his eyes closed. It was as if I could not speak or communicate, and I just stared at the wall on the other side of him. There was a sense of wrongness in what he was doing, especially because this was the first time he had undressed me, but we were all alone. I had no one to talk to or run to, nowhere to walk to and ask for help, and no one to confirm if what he was doing was normal. It certainly felt negative, but I was unable to speak.

In another sense, I did not question what he was doing, because he was my older brother, and I did not know if his actions were wrong. But it did indeed feel wrong. He continued to do whatever he pleased to me, but with his eyes closed, so he could not look at me in despair. He knew he was in the wrong, but I was not comprehending what he was doing to me physically. When he finally left me alone and fell asleep, I slipped out of his room, went back downstairs, and proceeded to watch television until someone arrived home.

I stared blankly at the television and saw an image of my father in my third eye. When I focused on the image in my clairvoyance field, I saw tears in his eyes. That afternoon once Mother arrived and locked herself in her room, I played outside with my neighbors until the streetlights came on. I did not say a word to anyone in the house, including Elma or my neighbors about what my brother did to me, and I kept it a secret. There was guilt in my soul for what he did, but on reflection, it was my soul refusing to accept that Chris engaged in sexual energy exchange with me.

In the following two years or so, the dynamics intensified between every person in the household, including our "parents," Elma and Mother. The house was increasingly stirring up negative energy, mainly due to circumstances such as residual energy from Geraldine, Mother's depression, and poor habits (drinking, smoking cigarettes, and whatever can numb her state of being), Chris's molesting, Giovanna's hostility towards us, and Elma's soon to come anger and explosive rage from everything being on her shoulders. It was evident that my mother neglecting us blindsided her to the constant tension between us children, but there is the possibility that she knew but did not care.

My mother was not aware of what her oldest son was doing to me, and potentially my sisters, God forbid. In her excessive absence, Chris easily could have targeted any one of us for his pleasure and sick desires to fulfill whatever dreams he had sexually. After repeated incidents of Chris taking advantage of me, it was certain that each time it worsened, and the frequency increased. After some time, I was certain that the same thing was happening to Anne and Giovanna, too, because they would sometimes disappear and all I could hear was music blaring from his room to cover up any other noise. Elma started locking herself in the bedroom more with my mother, because she was starting to hit rock-bottom from the stress in the household.

Days were similar in routine during this time, with a few exceptions. Essentially, we attended school during the day, did our homework quickly to have time to play with neighbors and friends until the streetlights came on, scrounged through the kitchen to make something for dinner, and sat in the house until it was time to sleep.

During the first grade, Elma and/or my mother registered my twin and me for recreational soccer on Saturdays. My twin played basketball after soccer season, and it was nice to watch her play in the gym on Sunday mornings. Although the soccer and basketball games were in town, Mother never made it to watch a game. My twin and I wanted to keep busy, since it seemed like only Elma desired to interact with us. After my father's death, my twin and I assumed that every time our mother laid eyes on us, she thought we were one of many reasons why her husband was no longer with us.

Elementary Years, Setting Foundation, and Grounding

During first grade, in becoming friends with Caroline and our neighbors, we were able to stay as busy as possible. Caroline came by my house at least once or twice a week, and sometimes she walked home with us from school. We played outside with the neighbors or in my yard before the streetlights came on. Similar to my situation with Mother, her mother was there, but her grandmother was the true guardian and enforcer. Caroline's grandma, who I will refer to as Grandma onward, was truly one of the nicest people I have ever encountered in my life. Sometimes when school let out, Grandma offered us a ride home, but we usually declined. My twin and I valued that time to walk home and gather thoughts, bounce ideas off one another, hang out with friends walking, and think through what we may come home to. Since we did not know what would occur that day, what my older siblings had up their sleeve to ruin our afternoon/evening, or what mood everyone in the house would carry, we wanted to prepare. It was in our best interest not to arrive home any faster than we needed to.

I remember the first time that Caroline's mother walked down the street to pick up Caroline. When she met my mother, it was a strange but strong connection, as if they knew each other from somewhere. Oddly, their interaction was not connective in a friendship way, but rather, they were distant and standoffish to one another. Caroline and I thought it was rather strange, but we did not put much thought into it. There were bigger fish to fry in our worlds, especially daily pure survival and staying happy in the interim.

Throughout the school year, I noticed that the girls in my classes had cute outfits and had their hair nicely done. Although my hair was slightly longer than an afro and growing, Mother took us to a hair salon in our hometown to get our hair trimmed. Luckily, Elma came with us for support. While we were there, one of the women working in the salon recommended that my hair should be styled through relaxing it, to manage my hair easily daily. Immediately, Elma turned around and demanded to Mother that my hair or my twin's hair will not be styled through relaxing. The stylist looked at my mother, and Elma proceeded to stand in between her and my mother as she exclaimed, "I said exactly that. These beautiful girls will not have their hair relaxed. If you cannot do anything else with their hair, you can do their mother's hair and leave the girls untouched." The salon workers did not touch our hair other than washing it and blow-drying it straight. Elma scorned them the entire time to ensure that nothing was done to our hair to relax the curls. Once we left the salon, Elma made it clear to Mother that our hair was sacred and people would die for our curls. She also insisted that our hair never be short ever again in addition to never having a service such as relaxing it or something else that chemically damaged hair.

Elma's protection over us was motherly, yet her energy on the surface was masculine based on the tone in which she spoke as well as how she dressed. She usually wore a wife beater, t-shirt, or a hoodie with basketball shorts and a baseball hat with the Woody the Woodpecker cartoon character. In addition to Elma's motherly tendencies of taking over cooking and cleaning when she could, I decided to alleviate one task from her and try to dress myself one morning before school. Wearing a purple shirt, green pants, and black sneakers, I entered the room where Elma was waiting with a hairbrush and hair ties to do my hair. She giggled, and said, "What are you wearing right now, are you wearing that to school?"

I shyly said, "Yes, I dressed myself. Do I look okay?"

She said, "No, but let's go back to your room and figure out what you're going to wear."

I took the lead to walk towards my bedroom, where Anne was getting dressed. Elma said to me, "Okay, one thing you have to keep in mind when getting dressed for the day is for any clothing you choose to wear to complement. The purple shirt does not match the green pants, but a color that matches this purple shirt such as jeans or neutral-color pants would work. Neutral means either black, white, or blue jeans."

She continued to explain how I should dress to look presentable for an occasion, and how to ensure clothes are not too tight or too loose. She reminded me that although I am young, I already have a beautiful body, and I'll need to be careful of predators as I get older.

I stared at her in thought of a predator already lurking in my household, my older brother. I wore a purple shirt and jeans to school that day, with a pair of white sneakers. Elma encouraged me to dress myself up for the day based on her original advice, and within a short time with some feedback on my attempts, I started dressing for the day independently. I was appreciative that Elma showed me how to dress for not only school, but also took the time to explain the importance of owning clothes to get dirty in for cooking or playing outside. My mother did not teach me these simple "rules" on how to dress or tell me that I need to be careful from the beginning on the severity of protecting my physical assets, as my physical attributes are targets on a female.

Regarding Mother, she seemed uninterested in conversations that I had with Elma in front of her in her bedroom. My mother would open her bedroom door about once every two weeks, but sometimes there were small streaks where I would see her twice a week. Usually, it was because of Mother coming out to use the restroom in our one-bathroom house, Saturday afternoon with groceries, and a bonus sighting would be us being allowed in her bedroom for one hour to watch "Who Wants to be a Millionaire." The most time we would spend with her in one sitting would be when my twin and I would go on random trips up to northern New Jersey. We travelled north with her and Elma to either see Elma's relatives, mother's coworkers, or other random friends who seemed to have no teeth and looked sleepy, or to visit my mother's male friend Chris.

This trip to northern New Jersey would typically occur on

the weekend or a day that Mother decided to take us out of school for the day. We usually followed the same routine, in that first we would go to Elma's sister's house to visit her sisters and son Bobby. Next, my mother would drive us across town to see her friends, and somewhere in between we'd go see her male friend Chris at a mechanic shop. Each trip filled me with immense disgust towards Mother when she would drag us around to wherever her random friends were, in the epicenter of the ghettos of Irvington, East Orange, Newark, and South Orange and show my twin and me off to them as if we were trophies. She repeatedly would say things like, "Aren't they so damn gorgeous?" or "I make some beautiful babies, don't you just want to eat them right up?" as she pinched our cheeks and kissed our faces. Her friends were uninformed of the truth that behind closed doors, she completely neglected us due to her own troubles in her soul. The pain Mother felt from Father's death changed my mother completely and disconnected her from the world. My mother had no desire to learn about us and understand our personalities or teach us anything that did not pertain to her checking our math homework (with which my twin and I did not need help). I was aware early on that Mother's spirit was in a dark place, not only due to her husband's death. She struggled in almost every aspect of life: spiritual, mental, emotional, and physical. How she perceived herself as a mother to her friends were hurtful to me, as it confused us in the question we always wanted to understand. Did she truly love her twin daughters, or did she not know what to do with us, since we were an unexpected addition to the family?

The first time that we met her friend Chris was towards the end of first grade at six years of age. We arrived at a mechanic shop in northern New Jersey behind some building, driving through an unpaved road of gravel to reach the area where he worked. Mother left us in the car while she got out to see if he was available. As my mother and Chris walked toward us, the other mechanics and onlookers in the vicinity stared at us.

The moment that I approached them, I locked eyes with Chris; I immediately knew that he was the one. He was most definitely my biological father. In looking at him, as we locked eyes, my soul felt connected with his, and I knew that our connection was more than in that moment. In my head, through clairaudience, I heard Kenneth say, "He is your real father. This is your dad, Carla."

I then locked my right hand with Chris in greeting, and I instantly saw the image of my father Kenneth standing to the right of me. This was the first instance of seeing Kenneth without my third eye or waking up from sleep. To be honest, I thought it was magnificent because this was a new way of seeing him in broad daylight, and I kept the secret to myself.

I was not afraid of him there with us, until Kenneth declared to me in a stern voice, "He is your real father, and I can no longer stop you from seeing him." I heard the phrase loud and clear, but seeing Kenneth's energy next to me indicated that he felt strongly about the matter. I felt like I betrayed Kenneth by being there, but there was also a feeling in my heart for opening and the truth. I knew that I was not Kenneth's child, because Anne and I did not have the same skin color as our siblings, and they always commented on our differences. Yet, I did not think that I would ever meet my biological father. Chris asked me questions such as my name, age, birthday, what grade I was currently in school, and others. He smiled and turned to speak to Mother.

I looked at my twin and I looked back at him. Throughout the remainder of our first visit, I did not mention what I received from Kenneth, but Chris kept staring at me, because he knew that I already knew.

Overall, in our home the spiritual and residual energy was unchanged. In addition to being terrified, knowing that my brother could target me at any time, the number of times the incidents happened increased in correlation to Mother's intensifying behavior. My mother started to stress eat, and we noticed this through her excessive weight gain. In the moments that I saw Mother around in the hallway, she sometimes went to the bathroom to fill up a breathing machine with water. Due to her declining health, she eventually had to purchase the machine to help her breathe through the night.

Elma was always on patrol when Mother was out of her room, inadvertently guarding her and telling us to leave her alone because she was not feeling well. To me, it seemed as if she was never feeling well. Elma would sidetrack us and ask if our rooms were clean, if the kitchen was clean, the dishes washed… it was Elma's tactic to keep from allowing us to "bother" our mother. Furthermore, Elma started to get comfortable and she started to put her hands on all four of us. The first time Elma beat us, it was a time when Mother was going to the bathroom and she did not want us to bother my mom. Elma was in the hallway and looked over to see that all our rooms were a complete mess. She started with Chris and Giovanna in complete rage, yelling at them, followed by hitting Giovanna with her bare hands in reprimand. She then proceeded toward our bedroom. My twin and I had a small cubby space under our large window, and we stuffed a lot of toys and dirty clothes in there. When I tried to see my mother momentarily, Elma grabbed my ear and carried me to my bedroom from the hallway to beat me, followed by my twin. It was as if my mother was a celebrity with top-notch security clearance, and we could never see her unless permitted.

On the other hand, there were moments in which Giovanna and Chris would go into the room and converse with Mother, and there was laughter or storytelling. My brother Chris spoke Italian with Mother a lot, conversing about history, and Giovanna would connect with my mother about playing guitar or other musical instruments. The one topic that the entire house collectively connected with was singing. We all loved to sing, and everyone had his or her favorite album in the house to sing. It was typical of Mother to have R&B music such as Boyz II Men, the Temptations, or Smokey Robinson playing in her locked bedroom. Amongst the children, we all loved Mariah Carey's music when our cousin Rob came to visit our house one day and played it in my brother's room. My cousin Rob was obsessed with her, and he convinced Chris once to enter a sweepstakes to win free tickets to her concert.

In the nighttime, I prayed for uninterrupted sleep and a good day following. I prayed to God and Kenneth every evening with my twin and asked for protection. Thankfully, my brother did not target us for his pleasure in the nighttime, because Elma was a light sleeper, and both of my older siblings would hang out and talk until late hours. They played piano, sang songs, talked about music, and sometimes tried to communicate with the spirits in the house. It was frightening because my twin and I just wanted to sleep, but they would be conjuring spirits with tools such as a Ouija board, a spell book, and a wand that Chris carved. We would ask them to keep it down sometimes, but they would literally tell us to kick rocks or to shut up. The dark spiritual entities and energies were always taunting everyone in the house, especially at night.

One night, Chris and Giovanna ended their nightly activities early and went to sleep. We were excited to get some rest; it was a once-in-a-million rarity that we were able to fall asleep early. Anne and I had bunk beds at the time, but she usually claimed the top bunk. That evening, we decided in order to avoid spiritual encounters, especially any negative energy throughout the night, to sleep together on the top bunk. As I was falling asleep on the top bunk and had started drifting to sleep, I heard a voice that said, "Open your eyes."

In fear of the voice that sounded strikingly like the male entity I encountered some time ago when I was scratched and lingering in the closet, I kept my eyes shut. A few moments passed, and I heard the command again. This time, the energy felt nearby, and my body started to feel the anxiety in my stomach. I remained in fear, but eyes remained shut, knowing that if I opened my eyes, I may see something on the ceiling or directly in my face.

A few moments later, Anne whispered, "Oh my God, Carla. Do not open your eyes." She for sure confirmed the presence of something, especially since I did not tell her that I was receiving the command to open my eyes. Seconds passed by, and I felt a strong force on my chest, crushing my lungs. It was as if someone placed a refrigerator on my petite seven-year-old body, and I was having trouble breathing. As I laid there gasping for air and unable to move, I opened my eyes, forgetting that I promised myself not to. There it was. A spirit, clearly a male, sitting on my chest, facing the window to my left. The spirit then turned and looked down at me as I gasped for air. I almost fainted when I saw him crushing me in pure torture. His eyes were completely black, and the grin on his face clearly indicated that he was here to wreak havoc again.

Anne yelled, "In the name of Jesus Christ, we rebuke this spirit now to send back to his realm," and I remembered looking at my twin in amazement that she knew what to say. In relief, I felt the energy start to lift from my lungs, and I looked up to see his spirit fading. I was no longer stuck in whatever that matrix of energy between the spirit and I was, and I started crying because I could breathe again. I thanked Anne, then asked her how she knew what to say.

She said, "I usually stay up after you and hear these two at night rebuking spirits all of the time. That is what they do, so I figured I'd try it to see if it works." I stared at her as I cried quietly, but then I thought about waking Mother for comfort. Anne then climbed down the bunk bed and helped me down. She walked in front of me as we marched to Mother's door. I yelled for Mother several times, and she finally opened the door. She cracked her door and asked me what was wrong. When I told her that a spirit tried to crush me, she went to the top of her dresser and grabbed a pink pill from one of her forty or so bottles there. She said boldly, "Here. Take the pill. It will make you go to sleep." Mother closed her door in our face, and I took the pill to fall asleep. I cried for about thirty minutes until the pill kicked in. The pill was Benadryl.

As the days passed on and the spiritual commotion increased at night, likely due to Chris and Giovanna conjuring with the spirits, Chris brought a friend over on a Friday night to stay up late and hang out. I usually stayed up late on Fridays with my twin because the chatter between my siblings and my brother's new friend did not stop. Clearly, they were having fun, and I decided why not me, too? I entered my brother's room and say hello to his new friend, Eric. Eric gladly said hello and explained that he met my brother when he was finishing high school. Eric happened to stumble into Chris along the way somewhere. It was clear that Eric and Chris enjoyed each other's company, and they were destined to be friends. I felt comfortable with my brother in Eric's presence, and he often asked me questions to gauge my intelligence and personality. It was different from the behavior I often receive from my older siblings or any older person I have met, so when he was around with my brother and I was not interrupting, I would pop around for a chat.

Caroline and I became good friends, and she was the only person allowed in my house of my friends according to Elma and Mother. There was something about the neighbors that Elma and mother were not fond of (I thought they were amazing and nice), but now that I am older, I realize it may have been for privacy. My neighbor friends could report to their parents on how unstable our house was, and Mother would have been judged for her lack of care.

Caroline always needed to be walked or driven to my house, so my twin and I would walk up to the corner. To Caroline's Grandma, we made it seem like Elma walked up to pick Caroline up. Anne and I quickly learned that there were three young boys living across the street from Caroline on the tail end of our U street. My twin and I noticed them one day when they were in the backyard jumping on the trampoline on our way to visit Caroline at her house. The second or third time they saw us, they invited us into their backyard to jump on the trampoline. My twin and I visited them to jump on the trampoline when we saw them outside on our way to see Caroline, but we did not have much of a relationship with them. After a few weeks of interaction, their father saw us walking up the street and came outside to tell us that they were moving. I do not recall seeing them in school, which leads me to the assumption that the time in which my twin and I interacted with them was in the summer before second grade.

Into our school year in the second grade, my twin and I played soccer again during the fall to keep busy, and life was day by day. My teacher at the time was Ms. Mary Keenan, and she was one of my favorite teachers that I ever had. She was my first-grade teacher, and I begged her to let me be in her class again. I specifically recall that she would ask me all the time if I was okay, and I often saw her car pass by when my twin and I used to walk home from school. I always reassured her things were fine, especially on days where I was falling asleep in class because of lack of sleep the night before.

One day Ms. Keenan invited me to come to her house to meet her cat, because she knew that I liked cats from interacting in class. I accepted her invitation, and we drove to the West End of town to meet her cat. When we arrived, my teacher asked me questions about Mother and our living situation because she heard about Kenneth's passing almost two years ago. I told her that we are all okay and I did not need anything from her per se, but I sincerely appreciated her thoughtfulness to ask me how things were at home. I knew that she brought me there to see if I had the freedom that she suspected, and she wanted to pull me outside of the school setting to check on me. She indicated that I was intelligent enough to understand what was going on with Mother and my family's pain, and she could tell how bright I was. Ms. Keenan asked me if my mother struggled with anything such as anger, being sad around the house, not being nice to us, or anything else that was out of the norm. I assured her that everything was fine, and my mother loved us very much. For the sake of my mother, I was concerned about the external perception of our household, but I was thankful that she sought my best interest and safety at home as her student.

This was the first incident in which an outsider indirectly inquired about my life at home. Although I was seven years of age, I understood that any information or sign to an outsider would trigger more digging and expose Mother. To me, this was a sign of trouble within my house. I knew that Mother was not a horrible person, but rather she was a woman in pain from her traumas and current circumstance. I did not want to be the scapegoat in our situation at home and give the perception of our living circumstances. I was joyful that school year because of Ms. Keenan's support at school, and in addition, my relationship with Elma became more trustworthy. Elma was the parent in my life by the time I was seven years old, and I knew that her main prerogative was about structure and trying to help Anne and I become as independent as we could. Elma knew that my mother would struggle to raise us if she was no longer around, and she surely felt defeated by the unexpected gift of Anne and I coming into this world.

Although the dynamic remained the same between us siblings, Eric's new presence seemed to influence the relationships and tension somehow. Whenever my older siblings said unkind or snarky comments to us, he would intervene and challenge them on what they were giving us a difficult time about. It was different because Eric was not our brother, but he quickly became like a brother through having our best interests at heart in the house. Eric was a few years older than Chris, and since I met him, the two of them did many stupid things together, such as pranks like lighting their farts on fire. However, they also did normal things together like listening to music on full blast throughout the house and singing to it, as well as playing video games. They listened to Boys II Men a lot and Chris played his piano alongside the music playing while Eric sang. It was an interesting duo to watch, but I wanted to learn how to play piano like Chris. Nicely enough, Chris started teaching me how to play piano on his keyboard when Eric was around. I was okay with Chris teaching me piano, because when Eric started coming around more, his abusive behavior decreased slightly. While I did not fully understand it, I tried to look past Chris's tendencies when the occurrences started slowing down.

Other than Chris being nice to me, there was an added benefit for Eric stopping by our house regularly. I started to notice that Mother came out of her bedroom more often, which I assume was to make it seem like she was not neglectful. I learned the piano from Chris quickly, as I began identifying notes on the keyboard then moving onto reading music. My mother saw that Chris was teaching me piano one time when she transiently popped out of the room, and she questioned me to see if I was tone deaf or not (being able to identify tones with sound). She smirked and said, "Well you're not tone deaf, that's good. You should always know the song that you are playing just in case you do not have the sheet music in front of you. You never know." As expected, she vanished. It was here that my journey with music started, with learning how to play basic songs on the piano such as "Für Elise" and "Canon in D." From there, I started learning how to read more advanced sheet music and playing more complicated pieces such as Mariah Carey hits. My favorite song of hers to play on the piano was "Love Takes Time."

It is important to mention that Elma and Eric got along, but I believe she was a little distant with him since he was not a member of the household. I valued them both because they were my two points of protection, and I often enjoyed seeing them in the same room interacting. Most of Elma's interactions in the house were with Mother and us twins. Elma may not have liked my other siblings as much as she enjoyed being around us, but she still gave us a tough time through beating us when deemed necessary by her. My heart always looked past the moments Elma put her hands on us because I knew it was to set us straight, and she never compromised our safety based on her actions.

At this time, I already learned from Elma how to dress myself, clean and recognize cleaning products, as well as load laundry into the washer machine. Elma taught us how to clean the bathroom and kitchen before the other rooms, for us to understand the art of cleaning. Once we learned how to clean the other rooms such as the living room and hallways, she explained the difference and significance of a wipe-down versus a full clean. Elma said to us, "You always start with the kitchen and bathroom because they are the most used spaces that people cook, shit, and eat in, and need to be cleaned properly. There is no doing a half-ass job on a bathroom, because this is where people shower and shit. The kitchen, because you eat in this space, you need to have the nooks and crannies clean to avoid critters."

She cleaned with us most of the time, but primarily she let us work our way up to the harder tasks in each room. The last thing Elma taught us how to clean was mop floors, because she knew that was a messy job. I imagine my twin and me using a mop at three feet, seven inches tall. It was quite a sight. Elma ended up going over the floor to sop up the excess water several times after she taught us, but over time we improved on our mopping skills. Either way, she thought it was funny and would give general feedback like, "You're doing a shitty job, give me the damn mop," or, "Okay, you're getting better at least," or, "Can you wring out the mop already? There's too much water on the floor!" Either way, it kept us busy learning how to take care of the house.

Once we learned how to clean rooms, on a Saturday morning she introduced us to preparing breakfast. The first thing Elma mentioned was that breakfast is the most important meal, not because it was the first meal of the day but rather because the American breakfast taught several cooking fundamentals. Elma mentioned that she also learned to cook breakfast first and made her way to lunch followed by dinner. We went through an entire carton of eggs that morning, but she taught us how to crack eggs without getting shells in the yolk, beating the egg with a fork, how to season, cook, and clean up the area we cooked in because eggs should be treated sensibly, like meat. It was a long morning, but quite exciting at that. We learned a lot that weekend, and we learned how to make bacon and pancakes the following weekend. It was the third weekend in which we made breakfast in full, and Elma asked us to make enough for everyone in the house. Chris and Giovanna came down to eat, and we made a tray to bring upstairs to Mother. She never came out of bed to celebrate our first breakfast prepared in full. That was okay with me, because I had Anne and Elma to celebrate with me.

As months went by, the arguments in the house increased between Elma and Chris. Chris was misbehaving in the way that most teenage boys without their parents' supervision would, with his best friend Eric usually. Then again, Chris was completely out of control in his actions in other situations mentioned previously. Chris started dating a girl named Michelle and started to sneak her into the house whenever Elma and my mother were in their room to have sex with her, either in his room or in the living room. It was so disgusting, because he did not care to hide what he was doing from his three younger sisters, and it seemed as if he was proud of what he was doing.

After a few times accidently catching them in the living room on the couch together, Giovanna walked into our room with anger and sincerity in her voice. She barely interacted with my twin and me, and for her to walk into our room with that facial expression concerned us. Giovanna said, "Is Chris touching you two?"

I looked at her, and slowly nodded.

She responded, "He did something to me, and seeing him doing that stuff to Michelle made me realize what he did to me. It was wrong. He wasn't supposed to do that to us." She burst into tears of anger, and she turned around to walk out of our room.

She knocked on Mother's door, and told Elma that Chris had a girl on the couch and was laying on top of her. Elma angrily went downstairs and demanded that Chris get off her now and for the girl to leave. Chris disgustingly insisted that he needed to finish, and he was not getting off her, and I remembered Michelle staring at Elma. My twin and I were behind the commotion looking on from the staircase, and quickly ran up the stairs when Elma grabbed Chris's shoulders and pulled him backwards to the floor. Elma started screaming at him about how disrespectful he was to not only her, but to us and this home.

Elma watched Michelle get dressed and leave the house, and she said to her on the way out, "If you come back to this house and

I find you two fucking on this couch, I will personally knock on your parents' door and tell them how you're disrespecting this house." Chris pushed Elma, and Elma shoved him back, and told him not to ever put his hands on an older woman. He proceeded to step closer to her, towering over her at six foot two. Elma looked up to his face and made it clear that she was not afraid of him. After the girl left, Elma went upstairs to Mother's bedroom and left the door open so that she could hear what was happening for the remainder of the night.

Mother never moved from her bed and simply said to Elma, "What happened?"

Elma told her what her son did, and she said, "Oh, okay. Well, what can we do? He is at that age where he is going to fuck. Let him do his business."

Elma started arguing with Mother and closed the door. It got quiet in their bedroom soon after, and I assume that my mother maybe took a Benadryl to force herself to sleep.

The energy in the house became increasingly uncanny from that evening forward due to several aspects. For starters, Giovanna confirmed that Chris was also abusing her and confronted us for an indication that he touched us, too. Giovanna did not tell Elma or Mother what she asked us, nor did she tell them that he was molesting us. In addition to our common issue in Chris's behavior, Elma approached Mother with a serious conversation that was necessary for mitigating Chris's behavior, and she couldn't care less. It was an uncomfortable thought in my brain at seven/eight years of age to process that Chris challenged Elma when she reprimanded him for doing something inappropriate and disrespectful. It made me wonder what else he was going to do, and who would help us when he got aggressive towards us women, including Elma? What power did my brother have over the women of the house, Elma, and Mother? There was no male or father figure to set him straight in his role as the oldest child and only son of Mother's. There was no one here to tell Chris that he should be protecting us as his little sisters instead of touching his little sisters and disrespecting his mother at his leisure.

The spiritual activity did not stop for my twin and me, but soon afterward, we would hear Eric, Giovanna, and Chris having spiritual encounters in the evening from Chris's bedroom. Giovanna was still speaking to Chris, as were we, because not only was he the one in control, but we were afraid. I heard the three of them talking in fear sometimes, stating that they could see a spirit and my brother was desperately trying to communicate. He always tested the waters.

The spiritual energy also got worse once the altercation between Elma and Chris caused an energy shift in the house. The shift in energy led to Elma and Chris not speaking when they walked past one another, and Elma started to carry a bat with her in every room throughout the house. She would silently walk around cleaning and keeping her mind busy. Sometimes she asked me to help her, but her presence reminded the household members of the situation that unfolded between her and Chris. There was more silence throughout the house because of their energy disconnection, as well as us three understanding that Chris was inappropriately doing sexual things to us.

One random day, Chris came home with two buckets of red paint and painted his entire bedroom red. He painted it without anyone noticing and kept the door closed. Eric came over one day and shouted from his doorway, "What the hell did you do to your room Chris, why did you paint it red?"

My twin and I ran up the stairs to see the new color of his walls. Chris glared at Eric and calmly said, "I changed the color in here. They told me to."

Eric turned around and stared at us blankly, then looked at Chris again and asked him, "Who is *they*?" but Chris ignored his question and walked out. My twin and I went to our bedroom and stared at one another in silence and shock regarding Chris's comment. We then overheard Chris return to his newly painted red bedroom and explain to Eric that he had been practicing black magic to connect and communicate with the others living in the house with us. We continued to listen as Chris provided Eric with more explanation, in which he indicated that the spirits have been trying to link with his energy. Chris described to Eric that he started to listen to the commands of the house spirits, and he acted accordingly based on the commands.

Eric told Chris that he was completely out of his mind, and that he did not think that he should be conjuring with the spirits anymore because they were clearly dangerous.

Eric said to Chris, "Spirit would not instruct someone to paint a room red like the color of hell and dark energy." Chris kept reiterating to Eric that everything was okay in the sense that he had control of what was going on, and he wanted to comply to keep the peace.

Eric did not respond, and the conversation dissipated quickly, as it seemed his input was not getting positive traction. It was evident to Eric that Chris struggled deeply with something within himself, which Eric knew would not be resolved in those moments. After a pause in silence as Chris cleaned up the painting material, Eric changed the subject and they continued their evening together, hanging out as buddies. Eric did not let Chris's thoughts in the moment deter their friendship that day, but it was a mental note for him in his relationship with Chris.

I valued Eric's character because his focus in any situation was on the bigger picture of tranquility and keeping his environment as calm as possible. Eric was not avid to confront someone or argue with an aggressive opinion, like my brother Chris. He would rather make the general statement and let it go as much as he could. From my observations, meeting Eric showed me that he preferred to joke around and remain aloof to the perspective of others, especially about his life at home. He did not speak much to anyone in the household about his personal life until many years later. However, during that time he felt out of place in his home and so he spent time with us to feel like he was around family.

I believe that Eric was like me in that he tried not to think of what he missed at home, but rather, he indirectly became a household member within our home. In the same way I visited Alana's home or other friends' homes to alleviate my internal pains and growth within me, he did the same. Eric had a younger brother named Dillan, and he was the same age as me. He and I had a few classes together throughout elementary school and high school. What I remember most about Dillan was that he was nerdy and sarcastic like me. He was extremely smart and through the years we challenged each other intellectually in class. Dillan and I never had a close connection outside of school, and he seemed distant whenever we interacted. In my opinion, it could have been because he believed that our family created distance in the relationship between him and Eric. Eric spent more time with us than he did at his home, and I was inadvertently thankful for his presence.

One thing I appreciated about Eric is that he had a distinct bond with each person in the house, including Elma somehow. Elma was not the kindest to others and came off intimidating to my friends. As for my relationship with Eric, he helped me with boosting my confidence with taking physical risks. For instance, when I taught myself to rollerblade in the driveway, Eric mentally pushed my confidence level to rollerblade in the street. In terms of riding bicycle, Giovanna tried to teach me how to ride a bike initially, but her temper got the best of her. Her teaching was not working for my learning method at the time, and we would argue rather than practice. It was not long before I noticed that Eric had a way of mediating the overall energy between anyone in the house, no matter how big or small.

Family and Friends: Second Grade

Throughout second grade, I enjoyed every ounce of my time with Ms. Keenan in class. I felt emotionally sheltered when I was in her classroom, as I sat in my chair every school day, learning new topics and subjects from an individual that cared for my wellbeing.

At home, Elma taught me how to cook different meals, such as kielbasa with rice, and different meats and side dishes. Elma taught me to cook with Italian and soul food-based seasoning, since these types of foods were often cooked between her and Mother.

Chris also taught me a few things, I must say, although he was problematic in the house overall. He perceived us sexually through eye contact, made comments about what we were wearing, and would vulgarly blurt out sexually derogatory adjectives at me when I was wearing a dress or something form-fitting. The three things that I have benefitted from via his existence, ever, are: the importance of garlic in my daily diet, being introduced to playing instruments via piano, and his encouragement to embrace my Italian side and language more. With Eric and Michelle around, Chris was occupied and would bring the keyboard downstairs into the common area for me to play piano at my leisure. Regarding my brother's girlfriend Michelle, she was allowed over after that incident, but all doors had to remain open and someone else had to be in the vicinity during the visit.

The inappropriateness of Chris's behavior continued whenever he chose to strike at random. Luckily, Chris began to prefer sleeping in and often overslept through his weekday alarms as well as the weekends. One Sunday morning that I will never forget, Elma was unsuccessful in waking Chris up, and she was reluctant to take higher measures in waking him up like Mother did, by pouring a bucket of water on him. He never did this to Mother, but the last time Elma poured water on Chris to get him out of bed, he not only woke up, but he began to strangle her. Anyway, that Sunday morning, Mother heard Elma yelling at him in attempts to wake him up, and she intervened. I was in the hallway, and I watched Mother go to Chris's room with her black bat to threaten him.

Elma was to the point where she completely ignored Chris in the house and made it obvious that she would not instigate any interaction with him. Elma knew that Chris did not respect her, and she rightfully did not care to mend their relationship. As mentioned above regarding Chris's behavior, the instances started to lessen as he got older and lazier. But it was not over, yet.

Towards the end of the school year, Mother had to attend an award ceremony for her job, and she asked her old students that she referred to as Treach and Kay Gee to babysit us. From what I remember, they drove down to our house to hang out with Mother and Elma as they prepared for the event that evening, but they did not babysit much as I was told by Mother. I recall Mother visiting them in northern New Jersey or them coming to her job to see her at the school several times, and being babysat, too. They were not the random friends with no teeth that I mentioned before, and Mother told me that they were rap artists of the '90s. During their last visit to our house, since no one was babysitting us, and I was able to cook simple meals or follow the directions on the back of microwavable food containers, I prepared dinner for Anne and myself that evening. It appeared that they only came to see Mother and pregame before the ceremony event. I mention this because it was one of the many curiosities of my mother's relationship to famous people, such as Treach and Kay Gee, who are notoriously members of the Naughty by Nature music group. Mother mentioned to me on their way to the house that evening that she also had a friendship with Whitney Houston before I was born. I did not understand why someone who worked in the school system in an urban city would have friendships with these people, but I nodded in acknowledgement of her statement. Especially since Mother did not bring many friends to her house, I memorized everyone she ever brought home or let us be around.

For instance, Mother had a friend who lived in western New Jersey whose name was Alaine. Based on the energy her friend Alaine exhibited, I knew that she was lesbian. When Mother would take us to visit Alaine and her spouse, Elma and Mother gave me the inkling that they may have been a couple, too. Their energy matched with the energy Alaine and her spouse showed. I wish that Mother told us if Elma was her girlfriend, but she never said a word about their relationship other than being best friends. Also, Mother had a friend named Adrianna, who was a nurse. She lived in Paterson, and she had a daughter and son named Alexa and Julian. That was about it. These friends of hers visited our home, but seeing two of the three Naughty by Nature members in our home was perplexing to me on that evening.

Later in life, my twin and I ran into Treach in 2017 while he was smoking a cigar near the Hudson River, looking towards the New York City skyline. When we approached him, he stared at us, and we reintroduced ourselves to him.

He yelled, "Oh my God, this is insane! You look so much like your mother! How is she? Please give me her number so I can call and visit her. She has been a big impact on my life."

My twin and I smiled, and Anne quickly responded, "She is doing okay. Okay, yeah give us your contact info and we will give it to her."

He hugged us tightly and asked for us to take a photo to capture the moment. When I saw the flash on the iPhone lens, I heard him say, "From now on, you call me Uncle Trigga. I will always be here for you two."

As the second-grade year rounded out, Mother decided to put us in summer camp, which happened to be located at our elementary school. Before and after the weeks during which we attended summer camp, Mother had Anne and me complete workbooks in the morning hours for the next grade level. She handed us each third-grade-level workbooks and told us to complete one section before we could play outside. My twin and I woke up super early to rush and complete the summer schoolwork. When we were permitted to go outside, Mother would lock herself in the bedroom. We wouldn't see her until the next morning or if she used the bathroom while we were around.

When summer camp started, I realized that it was a pleasant time away from home, but there were parts that were not so enjoyable, since my older sister Giovanna and Chris were with us. During this time, Mother taught summer school classes and often brought Elma with her to northern New Jersey to visit her family.

The four of us walked to summer camp each morning regardless of the weather conditions. I will never forget how hot and humid it was as we walked to summer camp and the profuse amount of sweat that flowed from me along the way. The sun felt as though it was giving me a tattoo, and I hid in the shade every moment I could. We typically spent the morning and afternoon in the sun, since there was not much shade in the field of the elementary school. I usually asked Chris and Giovanna if we could walk up Sanford Ave. instead of Norwood Ave., since there were more trees and fewer opportunities for the sun to pierce through me, but they always wanted to bask in the sun on the walk there.

At summer camp, the setup consisted of a makeshift area of shaded picnic tables for crafts and playing card games, in addition to some shade on the basketball court due to the building of the school. Chris and Giovanna would attend summer camp with their age group on one side of the field, and Anne and I were stationed with the younger group.

I enjoyed playing mancala with Caroline or my friend Frannie in the mornings, and typically finished the mornings by playing on the monkey bars. Mancala was a thought-forward process, and it reminded me of playing chess. My father Kenneth played chess with Chris when he was alive, and I recall watching them challenge one another during the game. There is a lot of thought involved in the game of chess, as it is quite strategic in that one must think both forward and backward. An individual must think ahead and piece scenarios together, which may lead to a chess piece being placed backward while moving forward conceptually. This notion of chess and thinking both forward and backward came to me the first time I played on the monkey bars in solitude.

It was my first time I tried to explore the monkey bars after witnessing a girl swinging from one of the red bars in the playground. There was a moment of stillness in the playground, and the space in the shaded area where games were being played on tables were limited. I wandered away from the tables and made my way to the playground. My time on the monkey bars started with minor confusion regarding how to hold myself up as I looked at the bars above my head, especially since the ground beneath me was so far down.

I climbed onto the platform and approached the genesis of the monkey bar route. Leaning slightly, I grabbed the first red bar in front of me and moved away from the platform, then I looked downward. I realized how short I was and how far my feet were dangling from the ground. I then saw the spirit of Kenneth standing on the woodchips to the right of me, but he did not come alone this time. There was an older woman standing with Kenneth, and she was smiling from ear to ear. They both looked content to see me, and to be able to share the first moment on the monkey bars with me. I felt the contentment through my clairsentience in conjunction with the warm sun beaming through the playground area. As I thought to ask him who the other woman was, I heard him say to me, *"Go ahead Carla, go the next bar. If you fall, you can up and try again. You will not know until you lift your hand and take your next step."*

I looked forward in nervousness and smiled. I knew he was there to encourage me to conquer my first take on the monkey bars and being in solitude while I did so. I lifted my right hand from the first bar and pushed my body forward to grab the next bar. They both smiled, and my father encouraged me to grab the subsequent bar with my left hand. Just after I grabbed the third bar from the platform, my hands started to hurt. I let go of the monkey bars and fell into the woodchips.

My father quickly said, *"See, that did not hurt, right? Let's go, try again! Maybe try to make it across the bars this time."*

I wiped the residual woodchips from my clothes and made my way back to the monkey bar platform. This time, I took my time and made my way across the monkey bars to the other side of the platform without falling. When I arrived at the other platform, I was relieved, but the mission was incomplete. Although my body was tired, I needed to pull myself to the platform with the remaining energy that stemmed from my arms and hands. Without thinking about how tired my arms were, I propelled my body forward onto the platform. I sat on the platform and rested for a moment, then I looked over at my father and the woman. The woman stepped forward and said, *"Hi Carla. I am your grandmother, nice to meet you,"* as Kenneth nodded in confirmation.

I instantly identified her as my maternal grandmother based on her energy as well as the dynamic between her and Kenneth. My grandmother's name was Giovanna, and she passed away almost a decade before I was brought here to Earth. Just as I was about to respond to my grandmother, a small girl walked up to me with a summer camp leader.

She introduced herself as Stephanie and invited me to play dodgeball with everyone else. I agreed to join, and proceeded walked away from my grandmother and Kenneth, knowing that I would finish the conversation with them another time.

On our walk home, while the four of us scorched in the afternoon sun, I replayed the moments on the monkey bars earlier that day. As I mentally processed my interaction with my deceased father and grandmother, I began to see the image of the playground, where I was earlier, in my third eye. Then, I heard a familiar male voice say to me, *"I wanted to show you the replay of what occurred earlier today with your father, in order to help you understand the power of getting up and trying again. The power of going through multiple rounds of trying to make it across. This is a symbol, and it relates to your life. I want you to apply what you learned today in everything you do onward. You will need to get up and try again many times in your lifetime. But I ask you to keep trying until you get across."*

I stared blankly into the pavement on the sidewalk as I walked alongside my siblings. I desired to know who I was speaking to.

Before I asked the spirit to identify itself using clairaudience, the image of the male standing in white light showed in my third eye. It looked like Jesus, but he looked a little different than what I had experienced as his face on the walls of the Catholic church.

I then asked, *"Is it really you, Jesus?"* and I looked down again at the pavement and smiled. I asked him again, and it felt like a warm embrace, as if someone placed a blanket around me. Even though it was summer, and I was walking under the beaming sun, this feeling of embracement was light yet comforting. His energy did not feel dangerous or unfamiliar like Kenneth's, like the spirits I have interacted with in the house.

He nodded and said, *"Yes, this is Jesus. It is me, Carla."*

I chuckled in nervousness because the energy felt surreal but uplifting. He smiled, then the image of him got detached. What perplexed me was the familiarity of his voice resonating when he spoke, as if I have spoken to him before. But in that moment, this was the first time seeing an image of him and hearing his voice. His voice was powerfully tranquil, yet light in energy when he spoke. Honestly, to hear advice from him in that moment felt more vital than anyone else I had in my life at the time.

I never mentioned the exchanges I had with anyone on the other side, the other realm, that day to anyone. As the evening passed, I secretly desired another connection with Jesus, but I immediately felt the guilt and greed in my spirit by asking for something like that. His presence was not a luxury, but rather, a duty in his divine timing, intertwined with mine. I was merely thankful that he stopped in for an introductory note of advice. I was thankful for just that, and as

Elma taught me, I should be thankful for what I am given, and I should never expect more from people. It is safe to say that my first time on the monkey bars was a lesson I learned about life through divine sources. Thank you.

The summer buzzed by and after summer camp ended, Mother made us start working on fourth-grade level workbooks because we finished the third-grade-level already. The one thing I can say that my mother did not lack in: giving us unlimited learning resources to keep us busy during the summertime.

In circling back to Chris and his behaviors, they were still happening, but predominately during the afternoons before my mom came home, on weekdays or on the weekend. Since I was not the only one impacted by what Chris was doing, his target victim during summer camp weeks depended on who was unable to escape the house after going inside to put our bags down. It was eerie how he never made obvious his next steps. He would not forcibly grab and carry one of us to his room, but rather he would do creeping gestures, such as holding a conversation in a room but blocking the doorway. Although two of the three girls were able to slip away and go outside to play with our neighbors, one of us would not be so lucky each day. Giovanna never mentioned her interactions with Chris after the day that Elma caught him and Michelle having sex on the couch, but collectively, I assumed that we all wished it would end soon.

Between the neglect from our mother, the uncomfortable relationship with Chris, our unpredictable relationship with Elma, and our comforting relationship with Eric, emotions stemming in my home life were a bit confusing.

FAMILY AND FRIENDS: SECOND GRADE

Visiting Pop

Just before school initiated for third grade, we travelled to southern New Jersey to see my maternal grandfather. I do not recall seeing him since Kenneth's funeral, which was likely due to how far he lived from us. His name was Michael Trotta, but we always called him Pop. He was in the Navy when he was younger, and his house was proudly decorated with sailor anchors. I remember Pop's love for the ocean, and how his house reflected his love for the Navy and the shore. I am sure my Aunt Fran, one of Mother's four little sisters, helped him with decorating and upkeep, because she lived next door to him.

My favorite thing about visiting his house was knowing that we were close to his house when I saw the A&P supermarket off the parkway exit, and I could smell the beach as we got closer to his street. I typically fell asleep during the trip to southern New Jersey and would wake up when we got off the exit or as we passed the A&P. My spirit knew that we were close by, and it was equally exciting each time we took the ride, and I knew we were approaching the destination. The two-hour drive gave me positive anticipation that I was going to have a moment away from Chris and Giovanna and spend time with my cousins around my age.

There were twelve of us children on Mother's side between my mother and her four siblings. Pop had a clock on his living room wall, and each grandchild had their face next to an hour of the day. I remembered that Anne and I were next to each other, because he organized the clock by oldest to youngest. My maternal Aunt Elena passed away from a drug overdose when I was one year old, but she left behind two children. One of the children was Rob, my cousin that loved Mariah Carey. Rob and his sister, Jackie, lived somewhere nearby Pop's house and resided with their father. My other maternal Aunt Kiara did not have children. My other two aunts, Debbie and Fran lived close to Pop and were usually around with their children when we were down to visit. I did not meet my Aunt Kiara until I was a teenager, which I will mention later in the second book.

Whenever we traveled to southern New Jersey to see Pop, we usually stayed at his house overnight for at least one night because of how far the drive was. Also, Mother wanted us to spend time with our cousins and our grandfather.

The first time we went to his house was a morning drive down to southern New Jersey. Mother, brother, and Elma packed the car and we travelled down for a few days without Elma. When we arrived at Pop's house, I was pleased to see him, but I was hungry at the same time. Giovanna suggested for us to go to the convenience store to grab some snacks for the stay. I thought it was a magnificent idea, and the three of us girls walked to the store a few blocks down. The neighborhood was quiet and peaceful, and the layout of the street reminded me of our house on Forestbrook Drive. The street he resided on was also a U-shaped street, which led to one of the busiest streets in town.

As we walked to the convenience store, I thought about how quiet and capacious the southern New Jersey town was compared to ours. It was as if we were in a totally different part of the country, because of how serene the neighborhood energy felt. Pop's house was three blocks from the Barnegat Bay, and whenever I was outside, I could feel the breeze coming from the shore. As the wind blew during our walk, I felt an alleviation of tension in my thoughts from all that was transpiring in the household. It disappeared and there was not a worry in the world. It was the last month of the summer break and it was quite hot, yet it was such a nice walk after such a long car ride.

When we arrived at the convenience store, the three of us entered in excitement to purchase snacks after the long trip. It was not long until the man behind the counter looked up and noticed us three walking around, scoping for snacks. I was in the back near the refrigerated doors when I felt a piercing sense of negativity beaming towards the back of my head. When I turned around to walk towards the front counter, I locked eyes with the male clerk. I confirmed that his energy was the negative feedback I received before, based on his facial expression and his defensive body language change. He stared at me as I walked towards him and he immediately shouted, "Get the hell out of my store, we do not allow your kind in my store, roaming around with no parents. No negros in my store! Where are your parents? Is this your little friend?" He looked over and pointed at Giovanna.

My sister immediately snapped back at him and said, "Those are my little sisters, how dare you talk to them like that. If you are kicking us out, then I'm not buying shit from you."

I knew that Giovanna quickly switched gears into her malicious side, and I felt bad for the clerk about what might happen next. She turned her body and kicked one of the shelves where the candy and gum were stored, and everything went tumbling to the floor. She learned that from karate class for sure. *Go Giovanna!*

She then yelled to us, "Let's go!" and we ran out of the store in the opposite direction of Pop's house.

As we were almost out of the parking lot, I looked back, and I saw him standing at the door with a rifle in his hand. I knew from watching cartoons like Yosemite Sam that he had a weapon in his hand that could seriously hurt, if not kill one of us.

Although the tables quickly turned after a wonderful walk to the store, I thought of two things as we ran in the opposite direction from Pop's house. The first thought was how the pain and insecurities within the white male clerk showed through his actions towards two innocent children mixed with what I know as "negro" heritage. My second thought was how this is a circumstance to keep in mind onward, especially since this could happen to Anne and me at any time because of our skin color. There was not much that I knew about my skin color other than seeing Chris, who technically was not confirmed to be my biological dad, is dark skinned. My mother or Elma did not teach Anne or me anything about my skin color, because the town in which we lived in had several mixed races with no racism that I observed to date. But seriously, the next time something like that happened, my twin and I might not be so lucky if in the wrong place at the wrong time.

We circled around on foot and made our way back to Pop's house. We did not stop running from the moment we left the store to Pop's house, and we arrived completely out of breath. Pop and Mother were catching up, talking about her work and how she was doing overall since Kenneth passed. They both turned around and looked at us to see what we purchased from the store, but they noticed that we were out of breath and did not have anything in hand.

Mother said, "What did you get from the store? It does not look like any of you bought anything. You have nothing in your hands."

Giovanna glared at my mother and irritably said, "The man at the store scared us out because he did not like the color of Carla and Anne's skin. He called them negros and said that he did not want them in his store."

My mother looked puzzled, and she glanced over at Pop to see his reaction. He narrowed his eyebrows, equally in confusion over the statement Giovanna made. Mother quickly responded to Giovanna, "Let's go back to that store right now! No one is going to talk to my kids like that. Get in the car, now!"

Mother drove to the store in a rage, and we all got out of the car upon arrival. My grandfather stayed behind because he did not want to interact or have confrontations with anyone in the neighborhood. He knew that Mother could handle the situation and left it alone. He also had a cigar in his mouth and was a few glasses of wine in before we left.

Mother instructed us three to walk into the store ahead of her, and she remained a second or two behind us as we walked in. The store clerk immediately started to yell at us again, and said, "Didn't I tell you that I don't like your kind? Get the fuck out of my store already, why in the hell are you here again? Get out of my store." He proceeded to walk angrily around the front counter toward us.

Mother was walking into the store as he was speaking and walked toward him to intercept. He had his rifle in his hand still, which expectedly caused Mother to react by shouting at the top of her lungs. She said, "And who the fuck is you to talk to my children like that? These are small kids, and this is a free country, so they can come in this store and buy whatever the fuck they want. You don't have a sign that says, 'No Coloreds' or 'No Negros', because you're not allowed to exclude any race in your store. So, what's the problem? And put your fucking gun away because you look stupid right now."

The man angrily waited for my mother to finish then said, "I don't like little kids in my store without their parents, especially little negros that can steal out of my store. I don't want them here, I said what I said. These two nigger babies of yours need to leave, I don't allow this kind in my store. And you, you're a nigger lover. Get the fuck out of my store too, bitch." He stepped closer to my mother and loaded a round in the chamber.

Knowing my mother, I expected exactly what she did next. She looked at him square in the face and said, "Go ahead, shoot me. I'll have your ass hung by a string in the New Jersey courtrooms. Do you know who the fuck I am? You must not know. Put that fucking gun down, now!"

Astonishingly, the male clerk put his gun down on the counter and stared at my mother.

My mother told us to leave, and Giovanna rushed us out of the store.

As I looked into the store window, I watched the clerk stare at my mother as tears filled his eyes from the guilt over what he said to her.

I have no idea what Mother did to break him down, but she was brave enough to stand up against him. Giovanna insisted that we should not go to the car to wait just in case, so we walked back to Pop's house on the main road. I assume Giovanna wanted us to walk back to Pop's because if something were to happen to Mother, she took action to protect the three of us by not sticking around.

Mother survived the interaction with the store clerk. When we were walking on the main road, she drove by and looked at us. Mother looked enraged as she continued to drive to Pop's house without picking us up. When we all arrived at the house, Pop had a worried facial expression as we entered. He was in the living room where we left him, smoking the same cigar. Pop sipped his glass of wine and turned down the music playing in the background. Mother looked at him and said, "Everything is alright, and there is nothing else to worry about. Let's enjoy the time together for the week or so that we are here."

Pop ordered pizza for us to eat right away and made the promise to cook something good tomorrow. My mother continued the evening unfazed by what happened earlier, and she spent time with her father and her sister next door.

As I went to bed that evening, I stared at the wall and thought about what happened. That day made me realize that I was defined as half acceptable and half not acceptable. Per the male clerk, with no correction made by Giovanna or my mother, I was half negro. I was not sure how that made a difference, because I was equally a human, as he was. The thought of how Giovanna and Chris did mention our differences in skin color and that we were half black a lot of the time to their friends or in the house came to mind. There was a common denominator in that they were not negro or black, but I was thinking there may have been more to this. I needed to understand why being part negro was such an issue. Who would have thought that just the color of my skin would make a man, and Giovanna and Chris in hindsight, be so upset?

For the remainder of the trip at Pop's house, I did not want to deter Mother's quality time with her dad and sisters, so I waited until we returned home to ask her about my identity. My focus redirected to spending time with our cousin Paul, who was the same age as me. We had lots of dry conversations with Paul that resulted in Anne and I attempting to interact, but we tried to enjoy the time with him. He was very private and didn't seem to want to get to know us. We also had our similar-aged cousin Lauren to spend time with, who was my Aunt Debbie's daughter. Lauren's older sister Alexis was Giovanna's age, and they had another sister a few years younger than everyone. Truthfully, we had only seen Debbie and her daughters a total of five times throughout my childhood, mainly on gatherings around birthdays and holidays. Either way, we went through the rest of our stay at Pop's with ease, and of course avoiding the convenience store a few blocks down. My mother went to the A&P supermarket the next morning and purchased a load of snacks for all of us, including the other cousins who visited while we were there.

Third Grade

When the third-grade school year started, I saw Caroline and my other friends on the first day. I met a girl in the waiting area outside who I immediately felt connected to because of our similar mannerisms and continuous giggling with those in our vicinity. She appeared to be blunter when she spoke than I was, but something about that made me want to be her friend. Her traits complemented my personality.

When she approached me initially, she said, "Hi, aren't you a twin? Carla and Anne? I remember you from preschool at West End. My name is Alana, do you remember me?"

I giggled and stared at her for a moment, and then the image of us playing on the school grounds during recess popped into my third eye. The memory of Alana's chemistry with mine came to mind with this vision. Like me, Alana was active and highly talkative with others, but she carried her energy differently than me. When I met her a few years prior, I quickly observed that she was selective in who she carried on conversations with and who she played with.

We walked side by side towards our classroom line and she said, "Carla, did you know that you are my first friend? I remember when we met in preschool, we both just turned three years old. Our birthdays are close together, and we were the youngest ones in our preschool class. Do you remember any of this?"

THIRD GRADE

I smiled as I gazed straight ahead into the crowd of students ahead of us, as I tried to locate the memory of initially meeting Alana. As I stared straight ahead, something spiritually different happened. I usually see Kenneth, or a spirit come forward to speak in front of me or in my third eye, but this view was new to me. As I gazed forward, a new window that formulated as the inner window within my third eye appeared. I still could see the crowd of students ahead on the edges of the new inner window, but this window took over my viewing screen of the world. As I focused on the inner viewing window, my brain was flashing through my memories to locate the exact moment that Alana and I had this interaction. I allowed the viewing window to continue, and I found the memory.

Within milliseconds of locating the memory, Alana said loudly, "Hello? Are you okay? Earth to Carla, what's up with you? It's too early in the morning for this mess. Anyhow, I will see you in line, we should get to the class line before we end up in the back of the line!"

I laughed and said, "Sorry Alana, I was just daydreaming. Let's go."

She said, "Carla, call me Lala, I prefer to be called that. Let's go, girl!"

As we made it to the line, I immediately felt a close bond with Alana through my clairsentience, as if we were sisters. I knew that her connection would stay around for years onward.

On the first day of class, I noticed that Alana and I equally loved school. She was as equally excited to learn as I was. Throughout the year, both of us were heavily engaged in what we were learning and participated continuously on all subject topics. Alana liked math and English a little more than me, but I loved history and science.

When it came to English, I thought that I was doing well, but my teacher consistently corrected my grammar and word usage throughout sentences. This may have been due to the use of the Italian language from Mother and Chris, who preferred to speak to me in Italian. I typically answered in English because I did not want to speak Italian in the house and get used to the language. I wanted the Italian language completely out of my head and unlearned because of the embarrassment of being called a WOP in kindergarten. Either way, I found that school and my new friend Alana kept my mind busy yet eager to learn more. I felt anxious about the scholastic overload yet excited as each school week passed, and by every quiz given to us.

During this time, I started recreational soccer again to keep myself busy, but I decided shortly after it commenced that it would be my last season. After school I wanted to hang out with Alana, Caroline, and my neighbors. It was not long after school started that I discovered how close Alana lived from me. She lived a block east from Forestbrook Drive, and we formed the shape of an obtuse triangle in the distance between my house, Caroline's house, and hers. The three of us became friends with a girl named Frannie who lived near our elementary school. My twin and I used to ride to her house to visit on our bicycles during the week or Saturdays.

When Alana and Caroline were available to come along, my twin and I transported them on the pegs on our BMX bikes if we weren't walking. My mother bought us each a bicycle the previous year for Christmas and Eric was nice enough to put pegs on our bikes. He was also a huge advocate of us getting around in addition to his desire for peace within the household. Eric and Elma shared the notion of teaching us to be independent as early as possible, but to also be happy children and have fun when possible. Eric got along with all my friends, and respected them equally, as he respected me. Eric's presence was like having an older brother around, and not a monster like Chris who was unpredictable in his mood and behavior.

On September 16, 1999, a tropical storm called Hurricane Floyd hit our town. Although the floods and major storm were predicted days in advance by the weather channel, the severe weather coming to our house was not. My mother and Elma were not prepared for the storm. When the day arrived for us to brace for Hurricane Floyd, we started the afternoon in silence, watching the storm from the windows of our house. In the bedroom that I shared with my twin, there was a huge bay window and two windows on each side. Anne and I were jumping on the bed in our room in excitement because we were home from school, but Elma asked us to get down.

She said, "You never know, something could happen, and you should not be close to the window." As my twin and I continued to jump on the bed in anticipation of another request from Elma to come down, we heard a vibrational shattering sound over our heads. BOOM!

Then, Elma screamed at us to get down and leave the bedroom completely. I turned around just as we were exiting, to see that one of the trees in front of our house fell onto our roof. The tree fell above our heads where we were jumping on the bed. Luckily, the tree did not come in through the roof, but Elma made it clear that we could not go in our room until permitted to.

Since my twin and I could not go into our room, we ventured to different parts of the house to find something to do. I went downstairs to the kitchen to look for a snack, because I was bored. Everyone around the house was in the common area downstairs during the storm. I walked to the corner of the house where the pantry was located to find something to snack on. As I stood there and looked at my snacking options, I immediately heard another loud, frightening noise from above my head. BOOM! I looked at the side door to the left of me, and I saw the branches from the fallen tree pressed against the window. Another tree hit the house, just below where I was standing near the pantry.

Elma yelled throughout the house, "Where is Carla? Another tree just hit the house!" I slowly walked away from the pantry area, in bafflement that I was in the vicinity of the second tree falling on the house. Luckily, no trees fell through the roof or walls of the house and no one was hurt. Our house was the last house on our street that was impacted terribly; all houses to the east of us like the Nobels' were untouched. There were leaves scattered and small branches throughout the street due to the winds, but the predominant damage stopped where we lived, at our spiritually unruly house. When looking at the map in the back of the book, it seemed as though the storm entered from the west direction and stopped at our house.

We went back to school a few days later, and life went back to normal, as if two trees did not fall on our house. Mother did not do anything about the tree for several months, until our elderly neighbor to our left side knocked on our door and asked for my mother. Chris opened the door and Elma popped her head out of my mother's bedroom to listen, but Elma did not want him to know that they were available. I looked past Elma to my mother in the bedroom, and Mother's eyes looked droopy. I will assume that my mother was high from something if she didn't just wake up from a nap, though at the time I was not aware of what it could be from.

My brother told our neighbor that my mother was sleeping. The man loudly projected towards the main staircase, "If you don't take care of this tree, I will call the town on you for not taking care of this property! I am trying to sell my house and you're not making this neighborhood look decent enough for my house to be sold next to this dump!"

As I stood in the upstairs hallway, I watched Elma as she listened to our neighbor shouting into the house, but she did not react. My inner window opened to show me a clairvoyant image of our neighbors' perceptions of us throughout the block. Elma looked at me as she closed the door to continue whatever was occurring in Mother's room. I looked down the stairs, and Chris told him to get off our property due to his rudeness.

Before Chris closed the door and turned around, I went into my room before he could see me. I was in the house with Giovanna, but I did not want him to find me, especially since he was angry. I went to my room and hid in the crawlspace under the window. I heard him talking to Giovanna as they walked up the stairs and they entered his room. When they went into his room, I slowly crawled out of the space and ran outside to find my twin. Escaping the house successfully felt like I avoided fighting a boss in a video game; but since the video game platform requires a player to finish the obstacle to move forward, I knew that the ordeal was not over. This game of Chris tagging one of us as his prey had not ended. As time passed during which he was doing inappropriate things to us, he became more aggressive. Maybe he thought that he was the man of the house and thus he could do as he pleased. I guess we will see how that worked out for him.

As mentioned previously, Mother periodically drove us to see her friend Chris, who, she had not told us yet, is our biological father. Ever since the time Anne and I first met Chris, he was working at a mechanic shop and he was super greasy. I'll never forget how rough his hands felt the first time I shook his hand; I never shook his hand to greet him after that. He knew by the second visit that I preferred to do a high-five, because when I saw him, he smiled and said, "I know you don't want to shake my hand since my hands are rough. Lotion is hard to come by over here."

Anyway, on our fourth or fifth visit to see Chris, we didn't go to the mechanic shop located on the random side street in northern New Jersey. I noticed we were going to a different location, because when my mother got off the highway, she did not cross the underpass to go into the main streets of the city. Instead, she rode along the outskirts of a second highway that ran perpendicular to the parkway. We then arrived at a building that had firetrucks in the parking lot. My mother brought us to a firehouse.

I was confused when we pulled into the firehouse, because there was a man with no shirt on hanging from a firetruck ladder. It looked as though there was a firefighter's photoshoot occurring in the parking lot, as the man was one of many firefighters, shirtless and covered in body oil. I looked down when the men stared at Mother's car circling the parking lot. My stomach churned physically because the men were shirtless, scoping Mother's car like sharks smelling blood in water.

Once we parked, Chris started walking towards Mother's car. He was wearing firefighter gear. He smiled as he looked at us in the back seat, and he opened the door for me. He said, "Hey little Carla, how is you doing?"

I smiled and said, "I am good."

He winked at me, then we all walked into the firehouse. He briefly gave us a tour of the firehouse and showed us the cat that the firehouse took care of. Chris explained that his shifts at the firehouse were twenty-four to forty-eight hours long, depending on the schedule, and sometimes there was downtime. I thought it was nice for the firefighters to have a pet to keep them company during downtime.

After he gave us a tour of the space and the inside of a firetruck, he buzzed us into a room that had a panoramic view of the outside. There were buttons and controls everywhere instead of desk space, as well as a controlman actively pressing buttons. It was the ultimate place for an eight-year-old, to maybe get the chance to press a button. The controlman turned around to ask if we wanted to do something fun, and I immediately knew that one of the hundreds of buttons in this room controlled something powerful.

My twin yelled, "Yeah! What cha got?" and I watched as the controlman told her to press a particular red button. It was labelled as *Red Light STOP* in faded pen on masking tape. She pressed it excitedly as we watched all the streetlights in front of the firehouse go red and the cars stopped suddenly.

There was a minute or two of silence, and the cars started to beep. The controlman laughed and pressed the button after he saw one car inch forward and drive through the red light in eagerness to continue with their day.

When we left for the day and drove home, I couldn't stop thinking about how much fun it was to visit Chris. It was so much more of an experience because I already knew he was my biological father. Chris was aligned with me on my hunch, and played along with the secret, especially since Mother did not know that I knew. It was okay like this for now, as it was nice to get to know who my real father was even if it was a secret at that time. Chris was a male figure who I was happy to see every few weeks because there was no one at home to be who Kenneth was to me.

Back at home, my twin and I would try to keep busy by playing outside until the lights came on.

My friend Alana had four brothers, and two of them were fraternal twins. Each of her siblings were about a year older than the other, and she was the baby of the family. Her twin brothers were in the same grade as Giovanna, and it was not long before her brothers started to come along when she visited us. We started going by their house to visit as well, and sometimes we brought Caroline with us. During the winter when it was cold and dreary, everyone would come to our house and hang out. From my recollection, my mother would come out of the room for a few minutes to say hello to everyone before disappearing again. She absolutely loved Alana and her brothers, similarly to Eric, in that she was okay with them in the house as company. We would typically play video games or board games in the house when it rained and snowed, but we were usually outside whenever possible. If it snowed, all of us powered through the town to make some cash shoveling snow. Although the cash was a bonus for Anne and me, it was also a great way to pass time and get out of the house.

In addition to the Lawson family, my twin started to hang out with some of the boys in school when Alana's brothers came by to hang out. My twin and I had a few friends that lived near our elementary school, within blocks from Eric and Dillan's house. We used to ride bikes to see them or walk to their houses to play on the elementary school field afterhours.

Either way, Anne wanted to hang out with the boys more than Alana and Caroline, because she did not want to do the things we did. Anne was not interested in girly activities like playing with Barbies, Polly Pockets, drawing our dream house in chalk, hopscotch, and double Dutch. Instead, she was into playing with Hot Wheels, destroying my Barbies, Ninja Turtles, G.I. Joe, her Game Boy, and sometimes her Mr. Potatohead. I had a Mrs. Potatohead doll. My mother got us the matching set a year prior for Christmas. It was as if Mother already knew that she was a tomboy and was likely going to remain that way, which is why she purchased Anne toys and gifts such as the above. Thankfully, Mother wasn't judgmental of Anne's unusual habits, such as trying to pee like a boy while she was potty-training or shopping in the boy's section at Kmart. Honestly, I truly believe that Mother did not care how Anne was going to grow up and what her preference would be, which in hindsight is comforting for Anne and me to be free in our preferences when the time came.

Negative Energies

In terms of the negative energy in the Forestbrook house and its eccentric paranormal activity, there were plenty of moments when fear arose in each person's eyes, hoping that the hauntings would stop. In addition to our own household experiencing fears unfathomable to most, our friends Eric, Alana, Caroline, and pretty much everyone else who came by to visit had their own experiences. There were moments where we would all be sitting in the living room playing video games and suddenly, we would see a flash of purple come from one side of the room. The television then shut off, and sparks emerged from the outlet where the television was plugged in. Other times, for instance, someone would be in the bathroom and the light was switched off with the literal switch. It was clear that a spirit was in the room and shut the light off, because when the light was turned back on, we could see the switch turn to the correct position. There have been countless times that my friends did not want to go to the bathroom, kitchen, or a different part of the house alone. The energy felt intense, but our friends chose to tolerate it because they wanted to spend time with us.

One time something creepy happened to Eric and Chris while they were in Chris's bedroom. Caroline was in the house with us, and we were grabbing some water before going back outside to play.

As we were exiting the kitchen walking towards the living room, we heard Eric yell aloud, "Chris, stop talking to that thing! You don't know what it is, and I can't even see it!"

My brother yelled, "I can't, he won't let me!" at the top of his lungs, and that's when we decided to run up the stairs to see what was happening. Keep in mind it was early evening during a weekday, so not only were the neighbors still in the street, ready to continue playing, they were in front of our house looking towards the front door.

With the front door open, one of the girls looked over as we ascended the staircase to my brother's room. Caroline and I arrived at the top of the stairs and looked towards my brother's room. There was Chris, standing in his blood red-colored room, facing the wall. Eric looked back at us, and Chris started to speak extremely fast. Chris's voice was hard to recognize as words, and it seemed as if he were speaking gibberish. Within seconds, before Eric spoke, Jesus came forward in front of me to the right. He was standing in between Chris and myself, and yet again, his liveliness immediately made me felt safe.

I looked at him and said aloud, "What do we do?"

Caroline looked at me, confused, and responded, "I don't know Carla, but do you see that bright white light in front of you?! I don't know what to fear right now!"

I widened my eyes as I looked at Caroline, who was on my left, and I realized that she could see the energy of Jesus, too. Although Caroline could not see that the energy resembled a person, she immediately saw something to the right of me at the same time as me. Jesus said, "Do not walk forward unless you feel it is okay to. I will move forward toward your brother, but this is your choice to stay or to leave."

I looked at Caroline, and I looked at Eric. Eric's eyes were wide open, and clearly, he was looking in the same direction that Jesus's spiritual energy was. The moment was too surreal to put into words as I realized during the mayhem, we all could see Jesus's presence to an extent in the same room. I looked around and smiled, but quickly refocused to the more significant task at hand, the circumstance before us in which Chris was behaving bizarrely.

The next moment, I looked at Eric, who refocused his energy to Chris. Chris started to yell louder and was banging his head on the wall in front of him.

Eric yelled, "Oh my God he's speaking ancient tongues. Chris, snap the fuck out of it!" Eric yelled for my mother, and then for Elma. It was as if Chris's room had soundproof walls to silence any noise projecting into the rest of the house, because no one came out of Mother's room. Caroline and I stared into his room as we stood behind Jesus, and then I heard my twin running up the stairs because she could hear the commotion from outside.

Anne grabbed my arm and said, "Let's go, we can't be here for this shit," as we ran down the stairs.

Caroline quickly followed us down, and said, "Wait for me!! But where are we going now?"

My twin said, "I don't know, but we need to leave." We started to run up the hill towards Caroline's house, since it made the most sense to run in that direction and drop her off. The streetlights were almost on, and I knew that Elma would yell for us to come inside from the bedroom window. As we got to the intersection of Delacy Ave. and Mountain Ave., we watched Caroline run across the busy street and into her house. My twin and I slowly walked back down the street towards our house, knowing that we may arrive home to a sticky or spiritually dark situation.

We knew that we could arrive to the following situations: Chris having done something stupid due to the strong spirits he was conjuring; Mother and/or Elma being out of the room trying to help Chris (not sure how); or Chris legitimately being taken over by the spirit.

When we arrived home, Elma was in the doorway with a belt in her hand, ready to beat us since we did not respond to her calling for us to come inside. Chris was still yelling, and he sounded exhausted and in agony while Mother was praying loudly in his room.

I told Elma that we walked Caroline home, but Elma snapped back and said, "And why would you be walking her home and not her mother?"

Elma whipped us on the back end of our bodies a few times and told us to sit down in the living room while she went upstairs to help Mother. My twin and I didn't care about the beating in that moment because we knew that whatever was unfolding upstairs was not good. Elma ran up the stairs, and we sat quietly to listen.

Giovanna was upstairs at this point, and Elma told her to stay in her room. As expected, Giovanna refused and said that she needed to know what was going on with her brother. Mother asked Elma to bring olive oil and holy water from her room, and my mother started to pray louder as I heard her preparing for her next move. My twin and I looked at each other and heard my brother loudly speaking in tongues, in the tone in which a spell is cast, as she put holy water on his temples. It sounded like Mother and Chris started wrestling on the floor, and I heard Mother instructing Giovanna to put olive oil on the walls.

The screaming got powerful yet terrifying between Chris and Mother, especially since we had no idea what language either of them were speaking in. None of the commotion sounded like the English language, or even Italian. Eric ran down the stairs and sat with us when he said, "I have never seen this shit before, I need to go home. This is too much in one day. I wasn't ready for this."

He didn't say much and continued to gaze at the floor as we heard Chris screaming about how much the holy water burned him, and how much he hated Mother. It was incredibly powerful to not only hear everything happening upstairs, but how intense the energy felt for the remainder of that night. It felt as though I was in the scene of a paranormal movie, but then I realized that it was happening in my house.

Somehow, after some time, Mother was able to stop Chris from speaking tongues and behaving strangely, as if he was possessed. It took over two hours from the moment Caroline and I went inside to when my mother got her son back to normal.

He was crying hysterically, and he kept apologizing for his behavior. Elma allowed us to go upstairs, and I heard Chris say to Mother as I walked into my room that he had no idea how he lost control of his interactions with the master spirit of the house. The thought of his words, "master spirit," as I entered my room made my bones shiver from the sincerity in which Chris spoke.

Eric was gone by then. When Chris finished babbling, Mother just nodded and asked him to have control when he communicated to the spirits. She walked out of his room, did not say goodnight to us, and went to her bedroom to end the night.

In reflection, it seemed as though Mother indirectly permitted him to speak to the spirits if he pleased. Based on Mother's lack of authority, she did not try to stop Chris from conjuring with the spirits at the Forestbrook house, nor did she care that he was. I recall how distraught Mother was reading the letter that Geraldine left a few years ago when we initially moved into the house. That memory of Mother reading the letter made me wonder what Mother cared about, and whether she cared to rectify the energy which resided in the house.

The next few days were abnormal, since it was difficult to stop replaying how my brother acted or what influenced him. Caroline and I not only saw what Chris did, but in unison with Eric, we saw Jesus in different perspectives, which they were not familiar with. Although I was more comfortable in his presence, I did not tell Caroline that I knew what it was, if it was a spirit, and who it was.

Caroline and I did not speak about what happened to Chris at school because we did not want anyone else to know, especially since we both had a difficult time trying to fathom what happened that day. Alana wasn't aware of what happened initially either, and we weren't sure if she would comprehend the inexplicable story if Caroline and I told her. It was not long after when the three of us had a moment together after school, and we sat in the grass on the field behind school grounds. There, I started to talk to them about how much I disliked Giovanna and Chris, and how Eric was a buffer for the awkward dynamics in the house. Caroline brought up to Alana that we experienced something in the house the other day with Chris, and she could not stop thinking about it ever since. She told Alana about Chris's strange behavior, and how we saw a white energetic "thing" between us and Chris in the hallway. She mentioned that Eric noticed this thing, too, and she didn't know where he came from. Caroline hinted to Alana that it felt like a dream when we all realized that we all saw the presence of white light, in addition to Chris, who was in a malicious state of mind.

Alana looked at me and said, "Did you know what was happening or why it happened? What was going through that head of yours?"

I looked at her and said, "Yeah, well ... you know the house is haunted, and Chris has been communicating with these spirits. For example, glasses shatter in front of us in the living room, the lights flicker on/off, and we see the switches move as if someone was standing there. Spirits are scratching and touching us. Giovanna is also trying to talk to the spirits ... there's too much. It's a lot. The other day was the first time ever that I saw Chris acting like that."

Alana looked at me and told me that it would be okay. She said, "This will change and get better. We will be there for you, no matter what."

Caroline and Alana did not circle back around to the white energetic "thing" due to their focus on Chris's behavior and the dynamic in the house. Alana eventually changed the subject, and we started talking about school projects coming up.

It was springtime in school when I was assigned a report to write on the rainforest. My twin was in a different class and was assigned a partner to work on a school project. Our project assignments were due at the end of April, and there was more than enough time to start the work. My twin had to start the work immediately since her project with her partner entailed a plan to grow a plant. Anne had to go over to the girl's house to set the experiment up and allow the plant needed for the project to start growing. The girl was named Morella, and she lived somewhat close to us. My twin and I would not be able to walk to her apartment complex, though, because we had to walk across a major highway, Route 22, to get to the apartment building. Elma did not want to go with us that day, which left us with asking Mother to drive us across the way to Morella's house. I asked Mother if I could come with her and Anne because I could help them with anything, and she agreed.

Truthfully, I did not want to take a chance to be home alone with my brother. Elma would have been at the house, but I was afraid that Chris would overpower her if she caught him pulling me into his room, or even worse.

When the three of us arrived at Morella's house, she accompanied her mother, Liona, to the door after buzzing us into the building. Mother wanted to leave and seemed hesitant as she walked into the kitchen. Once she was inside with us, she seemed more attentive. Once we entered the kitchen, Morella and Anne started talking as Mother and I waited. I sat down at the kitchen table with

Mother and looked around the room to avoid conversation with her. Moments passed by and we heard the entry door into the apartment open. It was a friend of Liona's, who we noticed when he walked into the kitchen. Mother immediately looked alert as this large African American male walked into the kitchen. Liona introduced the gentleman to us as Chad, and he stayed in the kitchen with us while Morella and Anne mapped out their project.

Almost instantly, Mother and Chad started talking in the kitchen. The next thing I knew, they started giggling as they learned about each other. I walked to the other side of the room where my twin was because I did not want to listen to Mother flirting with him. An hour after Anne finished her prep work with Morella, we finally left. Mother seemed happy that she stayed around with us at Morella's house as we took the short drive home that evening.

It was only a matter of time until Morella came to our house because she started hanging out with Anne. She knew Caroline and Alana from school, since our class had 222 students. At home, it was not long until Caroline and Morella started sleeping over. When Morella and Caroline slept over at our house, sometimes they came at separate times and sometimes they spent the night together. When they slept over, the paranormal activity at night was unchanged. And since the incident with Chris speaking in tongues had recently occurred, Caroline was attentive and nervous that Chris may act abnormally again. In the company of Caroline and/or Morella, most times there was movement of the bed underneath us, items dropping off dressers from across the room, eerie whispers such as name calling that we all would hear at the same time or waking up at the same time to see a spirit in the room. We usually woke up in unison, which was quite strange, but we were so aligned in our fears at night.

A Reckoning

A few weeks went by, and it was a Saturday morning when Elma and my mother left around eight o'clock in the morning to run whatever errands they usually do. That morning I accidently slept in, and I was the only one with Chris in the house when I woke up. My twin was outside riding her bicycle up and down the street, and Giovanna was hanging out with a friend in the street. It was around eleven in the morning, and I was secretly livid because I knew my lazy brother would be getting up around this time as well. There was a slim window for me to escape to outside, but given the creaky wood floors in our home, it was unlikely that I would succeed. Even still, I woke up quietly and changed my clothes to go outside. I put on a pair of shorts, a shirt, and tied my hair into a ponytail before I quietly exited my bedroom. Now keep in mind that my bedroom was adjacent to Chris's at the time, and Giovanna's bedroom was luckily on the other side of the hallway, near Mother's room. When I left my room to walk to the bathroom across the way, the door was cracked enough for us to lock eyes, as he was laying in the bed facing the hallway. His eyes were opened enough for me to know that he was awake, and I felt his energy piercing through his bedroom, through the door, and into my space in the hallway.

As I was peeing, I thought about how it would be feasible to escape the house successfully, because I was barefoot. Although I could go downstairs, I knew that I was not going to be fast enough to run outside if he was already outside the door. He could grab me on the way outside. It felt as though I was trapped in the bathroom with my overthinking and thoughts of already knowing what was about to happen. I was running out of time. Strangely enough, I felt uneasy but in an ambiguous way, I believed that I had control of the day's situation. I knew that the day would come when his behavior was exposed, and maybe today would be the day that he would be exposed somehow. Maybe it was because I was going to run outside barefoot and everyone would see him chasing me. Maybe if he was bold enough to try to pull me back into the house after I made it outside, someone would see him. Who knows, but either way I would make my attempt to go outside after sitting in the bathroom strategizing for a few minutes.

I opened the bathroom door and headed straight for the staircase in front of me. I did not look back or to the left where Chris's room was. It was absolutely chilling because I made it down about three or four steps before he'd already grabbed the back of my shirt to stop me. I winced because I felt my adrenaline pumping, and it was only a matter of time before I sat there, frozen in time because I was forced against my will to be whatever he wanted me to be in that moment. He dragged me by the back of my shirt, slightly ripping it and stretching it out as he pulled me into his room. I couldn't shed a single tear because I felt so numb and couldn't believe that it was happening again. Today felt different in the way he pulled me from the stairs all the way back to his room.

At this point, I was unsure how many times that Chris had done this to me, or to my other sisters. As he was undressing me, I angrily thought about how he got away with this almost every day and Mother has not stopped him in his tracks. How could she be so oblivious to everything that happened in this house, and careless about the things that were brought to her attention? I thought about how she must not care about my twin and me, but then I thought about how Giovanna was also going through the same thing. It was all a blur in my mind, but I remember I tried to think about anything else besides what was happening in that moment.

The next thing I remember, Chris grabbed my clothes and threw them onto the floor and told me to go under the bed. I heard the front door open downstairs, and it was my mother and Elma arriving home from their errands. He pushed me under the bed and jumped back into the bed as if he were still sleeping. There I was, under his bed naked, with my clothes bunched up next to me, and I was fearful about what could happen next. As mentioned before, Chris was the only male in this home, and he had overpowered Elma and Mother on many occasions. *How can I escape from under the bed without him going on a rampage and hurting one of us badly, and maybe even murdering one of us?*

Elma was the first one walking up the stairs, and I hear her saying loudly, "Carla? Where are you?" She walked into Chris's room and he was anxiously moving in the bed. She looked at Chris and said, "Where the fuck is Carla? She's not outside, and she's not here in the house. And you're here in the bed. Why do you not know where all of your sisters are?"

Chris said that he didn't know, and he just stared at her.

I felt the energy intensify between the two as I stared at her legs from under the bed. I knew that Elma would not be able to see me under the bed, but I knew that she was not leaving the room until he responded with my location. There was a moment of silence between Chris and Elma, and I felt that she may already have an idea of my whereabouts, since she was resistant to leave his bedroom.

Without thinking, I took my hair out of my ponytail and pushed the scrunchy from my hair into the middle of the bedroom floor. I moved up slightly and I noticed that she did not see the movement of the scrunchy fully. I felt the power within me to make it obvious to Elma that I was under Chris's bed, even as I was in fear of his control of me. I grabbed my underwear from the pile of clothes bunched under the bed alongside me and slid it across the floor directly to Elma's feet where she stood. By the time I made it to the edge where I could lock eyes with her, Elma looked down, and she immediately started shouting to Chris.

She told Mother to get upstairs right now and that she was going to kill Chris because he was sexually abusing his little sister. I have never heard her yell this loud and this angry, rightfully so.

Elma left the room when Mother came in, confused as expected, and she calmly said, "What's going on?"

Elma returned to the room with a towel in one hand and a bat in the other hand. She handed me a towel and asked me to come out from under the bed. Mother stared at my panties on the floor and started to piece together what was happening. Once I came out from under the bed, Elma flew across the room with the bat and swung at Chris.

Chris got hit once in the torso, and he grabbed the bat from her. Elma and Chris started arguing with one another, and she was able to get the bat from his grip. They started wrestling to the ground with the bat, and Mother finally jumped in to stop the confrontation. I stared from the doorway as I watched them wrestling for power, and I felt thankful but scared of what this meant for the house dynamics. I thought about how I would live in this house for the rest of my young life with Chris. At eight years old, I legally had another ten years to be home, at a minimum, before I could move out and be on my own. How was this living situation going to work?

Giovanna and Anne ran inside the house and up the stairs since they heard the commotion from outside in the street. Someone called the police; I assume it was one of the neighbors. Within five minutes, the police burst through the front doors without knocking and ran up the stairs. I started to cry in overwhelming emotion, as I had a single towel covering my body throughout the ordeal. It was a blessing that Elma finally caught Chris in the act, but the situation did not feel safe or finished.

The cops placed both Elma and Chris in handcuffs and separated them in two parts of the house. Although the police wanted to take Elma into custody because she started the altercation with the bat, Mother begged for them not to press charges. When the police left, Elma went into Mother's bedroom and closed the door for the remainder of the night. Mother sat in the room and spoke to

Chris for a few hours that night. She never asked me if I was okay, or if this was happening to Anne or Giovanna. The energy in the house was dark, dense, and eerie to say the least.

The next morning, on a Sunday, two representatives from Child Protective Services (CPS) knocked on our door after receiving the statement from the police. Mother was not prepared for their arrival; she assumed the situation would pass on its own somehow. When they arrived, she insisted that they did not need to come into the house, and it was not appropriate for them to show up unexpected. They explained to Mother that they can show up at any time based on the needs of the case and circumstances. CPS interviewed everyone in the house to understand if my sisters were also impacted by Chris's inappropriate behavior, the relationship dynamics between us siblings, and the supervision of Mother's children.

Mother gave bogus answers to insinuate that she was always around, and that this incident of her son's behavior only happened one time. I stared at her in rage. The anger was shooting through my veins because she played the part of a decent parent and that this behavior from her son was a one-time misunderstanding.

When CPS interviewed me, Mother was glaring at me from the other room to see if my answers were answered the same as hers. As I answered their inquiries on my wellbeing and care at home, I answered as close to Mother's replies as I could remember. The words coming out of my throat felt forced and superficial as I told them that Mother was great. My face physically began to hurt because of how much I fake-smiled. At one point, the male CPS worker standing next to Mother purposely distracted her and sparked a conversation about her pig fetuses on display between the living room and dining room.

As the woman from CPS completed her interview with me, I started to cry in overwhelming emotion. She looked concerned and asked if I was going to be alright.

I saw Mother refocus on me, as she glared at me again from the other room, and I said to the CPS representative, "Yes, thank you."

The two CPS personnel walked out, and Mother stared off into the floor for a few moments. I left her in the downstairs area staring at the floor and went about the rest of my day in anger over the lies that left my tongue into the ears of the CPS. The remainder of the day was spent in silence, as if everyone in the house was being punished.

From that day onward, Elma was out of the bedroom more to monitor every move my brother made. Elma verbally made the statement around this time that she wanted to leave everyone in the house, she immediately followed up in her statement that she needed to protect us until something was done about Chris's behavior.

A few days passed and the CPS representatives unexpectedly returned to the house. They instructed Mother to register us for therapy as a family and separately until further notice. She laughed in their faces and said, "Okay, whatever you say. Now get the fuck out of my house." She slammed the door in their face and went upstairs to her room.

That same day, I smelled something horrible coming from her room, as if there was plastic burning. I usually don't smell anything strong worth noting from her room, but it was truly strange. I leaned into the crack of my mother's door to make sure that I could hear movement or talking, and I heard her and Elma conversing. I knew that they were okay, but whatever they were doing in the bedroom smelled funny. I went to my bedroom and closed the door. I was not sure that the smell was, but I assumed it was that one of Elma's cigarettes burned strange, or she accidently burned plastic in the room that evening.

Family Therapy

It was not long until we had to go to therapy. I recall coming home from school and Mother was home, rushing around the house. It was rare to see her outside of the bedroom for an extended period in the afternoon or evenings, but this time she was getting dressed up for therapy. She was quickly applying makeup to her face, and there was a sense of urgency and nervousness coming from her as she tried so hard to look like a normal working mother. She demanded that we get dressed and get ready for therapy in an angered voice, and I changed my shirt into something presentable for someone I have never met before.

Elma stayed behind as Mother drove us to the therapist. She complained the entire time about how imprudent going to therapy was, how we do not need a middle person to handle the "accident" that happened, and how this will not change the dynamic in our family. I stared out of the window as I thought about how everything Mother said in fact was the opposite of what we needed, as she repeated herself to speak the words into existence. Mother honestly seemed to be in shock and was not handling the circumstances well. In observing Mother's track record of reacting to serious situations, to me it shows that she does not respond well and acts irrationally.

When we arrived at the therapist's office, I noticed the two CPS workers were in the waiting area, anticipating our arrival. The therapist was female, and I recall she was blonde, tall, and slim. She first spoke to me, Anne, and then Giovanna for a few minutes on separate terms to evaluate what transpired with Chris's inappropriate behavior.

My mother sat in the waiting room after the CPS representatives left and asked me what the therapist asked me.

I stared at Mother and said, "They asked me what happened. That's it."

She glared at me and I felt her negative energy stinging through my abdomen. We waited for the therapist to talk to all of us in one room so we could get it over with and go home. I wanted to go home and disappear, but I did not want to actually "disappear." There was an immense desire to be in the safety of my bedroom with my twin, with the door locked, quietly minding our business. The realization then appeared in my third eye that my home would ultimately not be safe until Chris left permanently.

Finally, the therapist called the entire family, including Mother, into the room. We walked in one by one and sat down. Chris and Mother were on one side of the room, Giovanna was in the middle, and me and my twin were on the other side.

The therapist reintroduced herself to us, and said, "Since I have spoken to each you individually, the next steps are to work through the emotions as a group."

Mother glared at her, then rolled her eyes. I clenched my jaw together in anticipation and looked down as I heard the therapist start her questioning. The therapist started with Anne and asked her if Chris touched her inappropriately. My twin answered yes, and she asked her to point where she was touched. My twin stared at her, and pointed in annoyance, due to the obvious response the therapist wanted to receive.

Then, the therapist went to me. She asked me if I was the person that was in the room with Chris when my mother's friend caught him, and I said yes.

She then turned to Chris and asked if he understood what he was doing to us. He replied, "Yes, I do."

Chris told her that he did not do it and they made him. She looked puzzled, and asked him, "Who is *they* ..." she paused, "that you are saying made you do this?"

And he said, "Them. The demons made me. They take over me and make me do this. I don't know what I am doing, but they take control of me."

The therapist looked concerned, and asked Chris who these demons were. He then said, "I can't give you a name. They were left in house when we moved in, and they are angry. I try to be nice and this is how they repay me."

She looked at my mother, and Mother had a baffled look to match the reaction the therapist was looking for. The therapist then said, "Is this true, Ms. Trotta?"

The therapist then looked at me with an emotionless facial expression to continue her job. She asked me, "What did you and Chris do that day in his bedroom?"

I gazed straight ahead and saw the inner viewing window pop up. This time, I was sorting through the memory bank embedded in my brain and soul for something I did not want to search for. There,

I found the memory replaying from the moment I woke up that morning, in hopes that I could escape the house before he woke up. I replayed how my mission failed when he pulled me from the staircase. Here I was again, looking through the viewing window, but observing a sickening memory that I no longer wanted to revert to.

It was clear to the therapist that I was replaying the memory in my head because I did not immediately respond to her question. The therapist knew that she triggered something, and I could see past my viewing window that she was giving me the unchanged, emotionless stare, awaiting my response. I closed the viewing screen and turned to glare at the therapist. I would imagine the memory replay occurred within ten seconds, because only the therapist noticed my delayed response.

Before I could respond, Mother then looked at the therapist and sternly said, "Alright, that's enough. We aren't doing this shit. This is fucking stupid. You want to ask my children invasive questions? No, let me be the one. I'm the one in charge here. You can't ask my children that. You stupid bitch, what would you even understand about this? Do you even have children? Did your husband commit suicide and you're trying to raise four children by yourself? How does this benefit them right now? Fuck this. Let's go. I'm not letting a stupid bimbo tell my kids how to feel."

I looked down in embarrassment, as she has yet again failed to surprise me with her ferociousness towards people. It was understandable why Mother felt uncomfortable, yet obviously she was embarrassed and ashamed to be in the room. However, her actions made the therapy session worse by directing her negative emotions towards the therapist trying to do her job. There could have been a simpler way for Mother to tell the therapist that her question was a little too direct for such a sensitive topic, but instead she shut the therapy session down completely.

Although I knew the question was invasive, I believed that it may have changed things if we got to the root cause and tried to get to the other side of this situation as a family.

In the car, I cried quietly as I stared out of the window because of Mother shutting down a potential moment for me to speak about my feelings, and the fact that I was going home to an unknown whirlpool of emotion stemming from everyone. I felt that Mother's parenting could have swayed either way, in that she could have started to be a parent and monitor us more, or she could remain the same by locking herself in her bedroom daily to avoid interaction with her children. I cried because we were about to enter the beginning of a traumatic childhood of living in a house post-molestation by our brother, with unknown emotions and repercussions from him.

What annoyed me the most during the drive home was the statement I replayed in my head that Chris made about the demons and evil spirits taking over him to cause this. In my opinion, I believed it was truly a scapegoat for his poor choices and sick thoughts toward his little sisters. Although Chris did undergo several altercations with the spirits and unidentified energy forces in the house, it did not sit right with my intuition that his words stemmed from truth. There was a sense of embarrassment coming from him, especially since he wanted to draw the attention on the dark spirits and unknown energy residually lingering in our home.

After that therapy session, I had to write my school report about the rainforest I mentioned earlier in the book, due in a few days. Luckily, the report was something to keep my mind occupied during this uneasy time. When we arrived home, I walked straight into my room and closed the door, just as everyone else in the house did. The door slams from the bedrooms echoed through the hallway in a prevailing way, channeling the anger from the evening venture. My twin and I usually closed our bedroom door at night to separate from the energetic disorder of the house in general, but the slammed doors on this evening created an enhancing, uncomfortable energy.

Elma was home, but she did not come out of the bedroom to greet anyone in the house when we arrived. I was not surprised, as I knew it was not personal to me but rather that she was not prepared to see Chris's face without attacking him.

I stared at my twin in defeat regarding what transpired at the therapist office earlier, and she looked at me in frustration. I whispered to Anne, "What do we do now? Do you think we are stuck with him in the room next to us forever?"

She glared at me and said, "How would I know, Carla, who knows what Mom is going to do?" as I stared at Anne in emptiness. We heard my mother abruptly open her bedroom door and enter the hallway. I widened my eyes and stared toward our bedroom door in anticipation of mother's plan of action. Mother walked into the bathroom to use the toilet while talking to Elma, but she started to raise her voice, as if she wanted everyone to hear her clearly.

I heard Mother clearly say to Elma, "And I should have told this stupid therapist that this shit happens almost all of the time. This is nothing, they're just kids. What do they know? Would they even remember this shit? Kids will be kids and do weird things. It is water under the bridge, and the relationship between Chris and his sisters will remain the same. I don't need a fucking therapist to tell them that, I can."

Mother unapologetically opened Giovanna's bedroom door, and I heard Giovanna yell at Mother, "What is your problem?"

It was a matter of seconds before Mother made her way to our room and busted through our door, too. Her energy felt unstable and frightening, as she locked eyes with us. Her eyes were loopy again and glassy. We watched her open Chris's door, a little less aggressively than ours, and asked everyone to come to the hallway.

She said, "Is there a problem with you all getting along? You are all siblings and y'all must talk to each other. You have no choice. Chris made a mistake, and we need to move on. You know, many years ago, when I was in my twenties, my car broke down on the side of the highway. I didn't have a phone, and this man saw me sitting there waiting alone, then he approached me. He raped me on the side of the fucking highway and had me pushed up against the guardrail as I stared at a ditch just below me. I could have died. I fought him off, and finally someone noticed, and he ran away on foot when the car pulled on the side of the highway."

I stared at her in confusion because I did not know what rape was.

Elma said, "Alright Viola, let's go back to the room."

We were all standing there speechless, yet Mother continued, "We need to move on. That therapy session was a waste of everyone's time, and I made sure that we left before that fucking bimbo said something else. I wanted to knock her teeth in for trying to get you to say something that was not true."

As I saw the image of what Mother went through in my viewing window, I figured out what rape was using the context and the images. Luckily, I recently learned in school that context clues are critical when there's an unfamiliar word said to you in a sentence. My energy state immediately felt uneven and completely outraged by her absence of thought in how she spoke on a sensitive topic.

I stared at Elma because I could not look at Mother without feeling the beam of heat radiating through my body.

Giovanna said to Mother, "Okay Mom, are we done?" and turned around before Mother had a chance to respond to her. She went to her room, then Chris turned around and went into his room. They both slammed the doors again, and Mother stared at the floor for about five seconds.

My twin and I were the only ones in the hallway when she said, "This shit happens all the time, you will get over it. This was your brother, and it was an accident that can be fixed."

Elma stared at us, then said, "Come on Viola, let's go." Anne pulled my arm, and we went back to our room for the rest of the night.

In my room, I cried in my bed because Mother's instability was devastating, from the moment Chris was caught by Elma until this moment, where she came out of her room with her eyes loopy and glassy, vomiting those words she couldn't take back. There was so much disconnect between Mother and her parenting skills, and it made me wonder if she loved us based on her lack of parenting. I felt a sense of helplessness from Elma not wanting to be involved in the situation, because she was usually unsuccessful in being an authority figure for Chris.

As I look back to the memory of that evening, it was the first night that I stayed up and thought deeply about my life from where it has been and where it could be. I kept thinking about how far I had to go until I could leave the house as an adult, and I was already facing the emotional lashes of not wanting to be a part of this family.

There was a lack of communication and truth in our mother, who was the supposed leader of the household. My brother was the only male and oldest child in the household, so it was also his responsibility to protect us and guide us through our upbringing. There was clearly a failure by two of the most important people in the household.

On the other hand, Elma was my mother's best friend or girlfriend, but she was limited in her options as an authoritative figure due to her own sanity and safety. I fully respected Elma's boundary in the house, and I was thankful that she wanted to stick around still.

Although Giovanna was the oldest female sibling and the middle child, her temper was extremely unpredictable. There was no way to trust her intent towards any situation, especially if it had to do with Chris. They were a team, and they stuck together at all costs. Giovanna was the person who I would prefer to be a friend, but I loved her from a distance due to her short fuse and negativity. In all my thoughts that evening, it was clear to me that the energy shift had yet again intensified since Kenneth took his life three years prior.

The next few weeks in school, I was quieter than normal because my mind would not stop processing what Chris had done to the family, Mother's reaction and lack of parenting, Elma's sense of helplessness throughout the situation, and how I was going to adjust to the energy dynamic for the future. What would be my outlet to keep my mind off what was going on at home?

Alana and Caroline knew something was wrong with me, but I could not bring myself to tell them what had transpired just yet. Truly, I was embarrassed, and I felt helpless because the leaders in my home that should be protecting me were in fact abusing me.

Within the same week, I had the rainforest report due and needed to work on it. I went to the library every day after school to try and make progress. In the library, I walked through the aisles of books in excitement because of how much information was sitting on the shelves. My focus was on reading for pleasure, and I had no desire to write about the rainforest. The report assignment felt forced; it was like how Mother and brother treated me terribly, yet I was forced to live in the house with them and "love" them.

The day before the report was due, I had about two sentences written down in my English notebook. My plan after school that day was to gather what I needed to complete my rainforest report and write it up at the computer station in the library. I walked there with many friends, including Anne, and we all separated at the library, as we always did. From there, I started walking the aisles. My train of thought traveled back to home and how desperately I did not want to return there every single day. I dreaded being home, and I would choose to be at school, in the library, with my friends outside, going for a bicycle ride, and pretty much anything else but being home. I preferred activities that did not involve being in the house and interacting with my family because of their negativity and instability. I then thought about my age again, and how long I would have to live there until I could legally leave. Ten years. *Chris is sixteen, so he is only two years away from eighteen if he chooses to leave the house.* However, there was uncertainty in his departure from the household. Wow.

I walked to the next aisle and remembered seeing a large book specifically about rainforests. I walked up to it and grabbed it. Afterward, I made my way to the computer station at the library. It was starting to get dark outside and I knew that Elma would be looking for my twin and me soon. I stared at the rainforest book and stared at the large IBM computer in front of me. Then, I browsed through the pages and found three sections in the book that were good enough for me to use the information from. I felt a rush go through my body because of the limited time remaining until tomorrow, when the report was due. Additionally, I knew that I had to be home soon, because it was beginning to get dark outside and the walk to my house was almost twenty minutes.

I stared at the pages that I chose to use within the large rainforest book, and I started retyping the words verbatim into my final report. I completely copied the information to complete my report and closed the large book to return to the library shelf. I changed a few words to make it seem as though a third grader wrote it, which probably did not matter, and printed out the pages. I retrieved the paper from the copier and went to the same aisle in the library where the large book was. There, I was able to quickly locate another large rainforest book to use as my point of reference for the report. When I finished writing the reference book down at the bottom of the printed page, I left the library and went home.

I handed in the report the next morning and received an F grade two weeks later for plagiarism. My teacher tried to call Mother but could not get in contact with her, and when I noticed the voicemail left on the house phone, I deleted it. My mother never checked the voicemail, and she never knew that I got an F on that paper. I got a C in the class, and she did not have much of a reaction towards it.

There was so much on my mind throughout this time in my life that I could not finish off the school year putting my best efforts forward. Although I loved school because it was fun to learn new subject material every year, I favored being away from home and using that time to think through my life and the next actions I may have to take when I arrived home that day.

Not long after I failed my third-grade rainforest report, Eric came by to visit everyone and he immediately noticed the dynamic through the body language of every person in the household. Eric picked up on the energy when he walked through the front door. It was clear that the house energy was not in a normal state through my body language and eye contact as I opened the front door for him.

He walked past me and nodded in understanding that my concerns would present themselves once he interacted with others in the house.

Within seconds, Elma walked up to him and said, "Do you know what your stupid-ass friend did to these girls, did he tell you anything?" She told Eric to follow him and they went outside to discuss it privately.

Several minutes later, Eric came inside with a serious yet infuriated face and walked directly upstairs to Chris. Eric told Chris that their relationship would never be the same, and no matter what, he would continue to come to the house to check up on everyone else. He looked at Chris in disappointment and said that he needed to walk out before he punched him in the face.

Chris told Eric to punch him since he wanted to, but Eric proceeded to walk downstairs and out of the house instead.

Elma's Illness

Summer before fourth grade was like the year prior, in that we attended summer school in addition to hanging out with Alana, Caroline, and others in different parts of town. I started to go to Alana's house more because I didn't want to play on the street of my house, but her home was ideal since it was close enough for Elma to be okay with it.

Towards the end of August, I came home from Alana's house one day and noticed that Elma was not there, and Mother was packing a small overnight bag to leave. Since Mother's bedroom was open, I walked in and asked her where Elma was. Mother continued to look down as she hurriedly packed and she said, "They just did a spinal tap on her and she may have meningitis. She wasn't feeling well, and I took her to the hospital. I needed to come home and pack a bag."

I looked at her and I said, "So you're leaving?"

She said, "Yeah, is that alight? I didn't know I had to ask you. She needs someone to be with her, she's scared."

I stared at her, ignored her comment, and walked to my bedroom. I expected Mother to follow me into the room to continue her smart remarks about her whereabouts, but she continued to pack the overnight bag and left into the night.

I told Anne what happened, and that I would not know what to do if Elma did not come home. I was terrified and worried. On the side of my bed with Anne, I asked God, Jesus, and whoever else that was of good intention who could hear me to make her better. I asked them to bring her home because I needed her.

I woke up early the next morning in anticipation of seeing Elma and Mother walking in the front door together. Mother walked through the door at six thirty a.m. without her, and she noticed me as I was sitting in the living room waiting for their arrival.

She looked at me and said, "Elma has meningitis, and they have to keep her in the hospital until she is better. Hopefully she should be home in a day or two." Mother walked upstairs and got ready for work, and then left.

Although I was saddened by the news that Elma has meningitis (as if I knew what that was, anyway), it was a strangely peaceful experience to see Mother in her calmest state. That moment was my realization that the morning time was best to catch her to connect with her. Moreover, it was the moment that I realized that there was a peaceful and kind woman buried inside of my mentally unstable mother. I have not encountered this state of being enough to know who Mother truly was, but I did know that the battle she fought within herself was just getting started.

When Mother went upstairs, I remembered that I had not seen my father's spirit in a while and asked for his presence. Maybe he was busy, because he did not stop by.

Mother was around a little more during those days and seemed to be normal, but she did not talk much. Mother is a talker by nature and through my observations, I always could hear her either talking to someone on the phone, to Elma, or to Giovanna and Chris whenever she let them into the room.

A day or two after the first day of the fourth grade, my mother picked up Elma and brought her home. Elma was happy to be home and hugged me when she arrived. I felt safe again, especially since I was unsure as to when Mother would start to behave "normally" and close herself away into her bedroom.

Early into the school year, Alana told me that fourth graders can now join chorus, and we could perform with the fifth graders at our elementary school. I joined the chorus group in excitement, especially since I loved to sing, like my friends did, and we decided to sign up together. Also, I wanted to use this time to break out of my shell in terms of my nervousness to sing in front of people. I mentioned earlier that my older siblings and Mother played musical instruments and were into singing. In turn, I fell in love with artists such as Whitney Houston, Mariah Carey, Lauren Hill, Toni Braxton, and male groups such as The Isley Brothers, Temptations, Boys II Men, and K-Ci & JoJo. I learned early on that singing was almost always judged by the listener, and people will stare at you once your voice starts to project. Singing was nerve-wracking and frightening for me when there were people staring at me when I sang, but if I turned around and sang to someone, I felt comfortable. The main reason I enjoyed singing was because of how it felt when I sang: it changed the vibrational force in my body when I pushed from my diaphragm, and it felt magical. Singing to me felt as though I was clearing pent-up energy through the power of my voice. For instance, if I was singing Whitney Houston, Mariah Carey, or En Vogue, the way I physically felt from my abdomen to my throat, then to my face and head space, was something unexplainable. Singing was essentially therapeutic to me, in a similar way that being physically active was beneficial to me from an early age.

That school year, I was at an advantage that more friends were entering in my life and my relationship was getting stronger with Elma. I met a new friend named Sammie who lived between Caroline and Alana's house, and we started going to her house since she wasn't allowed outside during the weekdays. Our time outside balanced between visiting her, going to Alana's street because she lived next to a 7-Eleven store, riding bicycles across town to see other friends, and who knows what else. We even started to gather on the wood trail on the creek between my house and Alana's late at night to play manhunt throughout the perimeter of our street blocks.

Elma and I spent more time together after she came home from the hospital, and she started to teach me more about functioning independently. I have naturally curly hair, and it needed to be brushed from the bottom up with a detangling brush. Elma elaborated on how my hair should be styled depending on the occasion, such as for school or going to family gatherings. Elma also showed me show to make a part in my hair, how to do my hair in pigtails, how to brush my hair using a certain hairbrush to tie my hair back, and other styles to keep the hairstyles interesting. She reminded me to avoid perming or relaxing my hair at all costs.

As Elma and I spent more time together, I was able to physically be in Mother's room more. Mother seemed to be okay with it, and this also led to Anne being in the room with us, too. Mother played her favorite music, and we danced and sang with them. On two or three occasions, Anne, Giovanna, and I did mini concerts in the room, and they seemed to love it. Chris was barely home because Elma made him feel uncomfortable in the house, since she knew that Anne and I especially did not want him around. On the other hand, Giovanna did not seem to care about what happened with Chris, because she and him stuck together as if nothing happened between them.

Truthfully, since Elma came out of the hospital after recovering from meningitis, she became increasingly vocal about how she felt towards everyone in the house, as well as intrusively expressing anger towards certain individuals. The arguments started with Chris and Giovanna. They were insubordinate to Elma when she asked them to clean up their rooms or pick up after themselves throughout the house. At this point, Elma took a different approach, because they both ignored her when she spoke. Her new method was to stand in the hallway and start yelling about their disobedience towards her, reiterating that she is trying to help them become independent and better prepare them for adulthood. The yelling usually led to Mother coming to the hallway from her bedroom, clearly under the influence of something, with a powerless stare through her loopy, glassy, intoxicated eyes. Mother's eyes clearly signaled to me that she was not mentally cognizant of Elma's explosive anger and her older children challenging her authority. Their arguments were frequent since Elma came out of the hospital, and it typically revolved around the same issue. Clearly, there was built-up rage coming from Elma due to the lack of respect Chris and Giovanna had for her, as well as their loyalty to respecting their mother only as an authoritative figure.

Elma's bottled anger was released towards the house more often, and sometimes she was holding her favorite black bat while doing so. Around this time, I observed a new trait that Elma had, which was white film coming from her mouth when she yelled, unlike before. This white film stemming from her mouth when she raised her voice made it evident to me that there was a decline in physical health in addition to her apparent mental and emotional health. Each time Elma unleashed her fury towards someone in the house, which became more frequent at this point, the white film was inevitably there, and I could not steer my focus away from it. Something about the white film in her mouth concerned me. I felt drawn to understand what this could mean to her health, and why no one else I had ever crossed paths with in my nine years of life exhibited similar traits.

One morning, Mother was already gone, and I went into my mother's room to finish getting ready while Elma watched the news. I looked over to the garbage bin, and I noticed huge chunks of curly hair in the garbage bin. I knew that when someone is combing or styling their hair, some hair may fall out, as expected. However, the amount of hair that I saw in the garbage bin was much more than expected from a day of combing, and it was all in a ball, as if it came from one session of hair combing. It was unmistakably Elma's hair, and the garbage bin was not full enough for it to be considered a few days' worth of hair. I looked over to Elma to see if she noticed my concern for her hair, but she was staring at the television. I could not see her hair as she watched television because she had a Woody the Woodpecker hat on, which indicated to me that she did not want anyone to see how much hair she was losing.

My viewing window opened, and I saw an image of an older woman with soft features in her face who seemed to have aged well. I did not recognize this woman, and she did not frighten me when her face appeared. Her energy reminded me of Elma's, so I assumed it was a family member of hers. The energy of this older woman irradiated wisdom yet delicacy in her voice as she said, "Her hair loss and her dry mouth are directly related to her health, and she is angry about it. You must be docile with her during this time, and patient with her throughout this time in her life. They do not care to see it, but you do. Stay close to her." I saw the viewing window disappear and stared at the mirror in front of me. I lowered my eyebrows in sadness at the message, but in confirmation that my inkling on her changes in physical attributes meant something serious.

I looked over to Elma on my left, and she redirected her focus from the television to me. She said, "Let's go," and we headed off to school.

Thanksgiving rolled around and on the morning of, my mother realized that she did not take the turkey out of the freezer. She knew that she had to run out to the supermarket. I was not surprised to be awakened by the sound of Mother's chaos and loud rambling in the kitchen about her accidently not taking the turkey out of the freezer. It was completely her fault, since we were unaware that she was going to cook Thanksgiving that year. We typically go to Pop's house, or next door to my Aunt Fran's, but at home we would not gather for the meal. Mother left the house enraged and started driving away in the direction of Caroline's house. I looked out of the window in awe about her enraged anger over not taking a turkey out to thaw. As she began to drive uphill, she started to cut onto the other side of the road, and I could not see her car anymore. Then suddenly, I heard BOOM! Certainly, it sounded as though her car crashed into something, but it was unfeasible to tell what occurred due to the parked cars on the street blocking my view. I yelled to Elma that something happened to Mother.

Before Elma and I made it out of the house, we could hear Mother arguing with the next-door neighbor, Alvin. He was rightfully yelling at Mother for carelessly driving on the other side of the road and not being mindful of her driving. My mother said, "I was trying to avoid the pile of leaves on my side of the street because the edges are slippery. I'm truly sorry, Alvin. Can we avoid filing this with our insurances?"

As Elma and I walked towards her, Alvin's two children and wife came outside to see the commotion. Alvin exclaimed, "You broke my finger, you destroyed my car! How in God's name do you think you will get away with crashing into my car head on, destroying it, and breaking my finger without paying for what you did?"

She stared at him in silence and did not say anything in response. Mother saw us approach and looked at me, and then looked at Elma. She said, "Well, I guess we aren't having a turkey for Thanksgiving dinner. Take something out of the freezer."

Elma looked at her and nodded. We left her in the street arguing with Alvin as we turned around to walk towards the house. We could hear Mother cussing herself out every few seconds in regret for her actions. I honestly felt terrible for her to start her Thanksgiving morning like that, and I was hopeful that we could have a nice dinner if I helped Mother cook.

Mother was so distraught from the car accident with our next-door neighbor that we ended up eating leftovers from the refrigerator. My mother went to her bedroom with Elma for the remainder of the holiday, and we scavenged through the fridge to find something. Happy Thanksgiving.

The time started to move faster, and Christmas break from school approached. The chorus concert was a success, midterm examinations went well, and it was time for us to start Christmas break. Everyone in the household was home throughout the winter break, and we had friends come over to hang out and play video games. Alana and her brothers visited, Morella, Caroline, Eric visited pretty much every day, and sometimes Giovanna invited her new friend Melissa to visit the house. No one slept over during this timeframe in my recollection, because a lot of the fighting between Elma and my older siblings, with Mother's clueless intervening while loopy and glassy-eyed, reoccurred the most.

A few days before Christmas, Giovanna started an argument with Elma because she was fed up with the authoritative commands towards her. Giovanna was eleven years old, and I will never forget when she purposely spoke loudly from the living room and said that Elma was a bald bitch that thinks she is our parent, and no one will replace her father because he's dead.

Elma stormed into the living room with a cheese grater in her hand. She asked Giovanna to repeat what she said.

Giovanna told her, "You have no right to tell me or any of us what to do anymore, you're not our parent."

Elma said, "No, I said to repeat what the fuck you just said. Say it!"

Giovanna stared at her, and exclaimed, "You're not our mother, you bald bitch!" Within seconds, Elma grabbed her arm and pressed the cheese grater along her arm, completely removing chunks of skin, as if she was a block of cheese.

Anne and I stared at Elma in bewilderment because this behavior was not typical of Elma. We had been beaten with hairbrushes, belts, and metal spatulas, but never had we been skinned with a cheese grater! Giovanna screamed in fright and in pain, knowing that she got under Elma's skin with what she said. Literally speaking, Elma reciprocated the energy she felt from Giovanna's offensive statement and skinned her entire forearm with a cheese grater.

My twin and I were frozen, and we were unsure if we should walk out of the living room or stay there. We stayed there as

Giovanna ran out of the room and upstairs to Mother's room, screaming. She banged on Mother's door, and she did not answer.

Rolling with the Punches

Christmas was ambiguously stressful, since the family did not want to gather around the Christmas tree together. Mother fixated on forcing us to sit together in our holiday pajamas on Christmas Eve while she took photos of us. Mother nudged us one by one as she insisted on making us pose, taking photos of us as if we truly loved each other and enjoyed each other's company.

Mother wanted us to appear joyous, even though I was uneasy with everyone in the household except for my twin. Our relationship was solid because we both shared a room and were in unison, which created an outlet for the physical, emotional, mental, and spiritual madness in the Trotta household. It was my twin and me against the rest of the house, with Elma on our side when she wasn't manically yelling at everyone in the house to release the stress that she was going through with presumably her health.

Although I was not totally sure of the status of Elma's health, I knew that she was not as healthy since she returned from the hospital. Her hair was falling out, and she wore any type of head covering, such as a bandana, in addition to her hat when going outside of the home. Elma's anger intensified, as if there were chemical changes occurring in her brain by the way she completely snapped into a woman of pure anger as she reacted to the words and body language received from others. Her eyes were dull when we locked eyes with one another in conversation, and she was frailer as the months went by since the last hospital visit.

A few days after Christmas, I woke up one early morning to see that Elma was gone again and Mother was awake. It was around seven o'clock in the morning, and as I exited the bathroom, I noticed Mother's bedroom door was ajar. As I locked eyes with her, I immediately saw my inner window appear in my third eye. The image was of Elma in the middle of the night, talking to Mother about her high fever and symptoms like the last time she had meningitis. Mother knew that she may have meningitis again and insisted on taking Elma back to the hospital. She did not fight Mother's notion this time, even though Elma knew that she may have to undergo another spinal tap.

The window vanished and I found myself looking at Mother. I asked her if Elma went back to the hospital because she was feeling ill again. Mother nodded and insisted that Elma was strong and would be okay. Mother turned away from me to watch the morning news and went about her day in silence.

I waited patiently for Elma to arrive home each day while I maintained my hair, cooked dinner for myself and Anne, cleaned my room and clothes based on what she'd taught me. Using what I have learned to survive each day, I tried my best to not think about the change in the household energy due to her absence. I was gloomy because her absence deeply impacted my feelings of safety and security in the household, especially since her absence could mean an opportunity for Chris to strike again. Thankfully, he didn't attempt anything.

This time around, Elma was in the hospital for almost two weeks. Just like the last time Elma was in the hospital, Mother visited Elma alone and never brought any of her children along. When Elma arrived home, she remained bedridden for a few days until she was strong enough to move around. Elma did not move around the house much afterward, and she rarely went downstairs for something. Mother and I took turns bringing her whatever she needed to ensure she recovered as best as she possibly could. After Mother felt comfortable with how I followed Elma's instructions, she fully relied on me to take care of Elma in terms of food and comfort.

After a week or so, Mother and Elma got into an intense argument in the bedroom. I overheard the yelling from my bedroom, and I heard Elma leave the house. I was unsure of where Elma was headed to as I watched her from my bedroom window, but she exited the house with a backpack. Based on her habits of traveling by train to northern New Jersey, she likely walked to the Plainfield train station across town. There was an uneasy feeling in my stomach as I watched her make her way up Sanford without hesitation or turning back. I was nervous due to her fragility throughout the past few weeks and months, but I was also distressed to be alone in the house again. There was a sense of relief that Elma stood up for herself and chose her sanity over staying in the house with us. However, there was a sense of sorrow because she left the house without saying anything to me.

Two days later, I woke up around six a.m. and started watching cartoons in the living room in solitude. Everyone was sleeping, and as I stared at the TV screen in the living room, I felt an energy presence. I looked around the room but did not see anything out of the ordinary. I stood up from the floor and walked towards the front door. I approached the door and looked at the window to see Elma standing there in silence. My claircognizance kicked in, because I knew she was there before I saw her.

Elma must have left her key behind, because it was too cold for her to be standing outside in the dead of winter. I immediately opened the door to let her in, and she walked past me without greeting me. As I closed the front door, I peeped outside to see her friend Stephanie in the driveway, waiting in the car.

I stared at Elma as she stormed in the kitchen, because she did not greet me. I felt the intensity of her energy presented upon her arrival, and I did not do anything for her to be this livid. Her energy filled the room with anger and focused on her mission to get in and out of the house. She was done with Mother and us. In the kitchen, Elma grabbed a glass and proceeded to the sink to grab some tap water, then walked past me a second time towards the front door. For a split second I thought that she was going to leave again, but she turned and proceeded up the staircase. She opened my mother's bedroom door and went inside. I did not go upstairs because I knew that Elma would return downstairs soon. Her friend was waiting outside with the car engine still running. She was grabbing more things.

Elma's energy deflected onto me in a way that I could feel that day was going to be the last transaction I would ever have with her. My clairsentience was heightened with hers. I was not sure what was ahead because I could not see visions farther in the future, yet, but I patiently waited for her return downstairs so that I could say goodbye.

I stood at the bottom of the staircase and waited for Elma to come out of Mother's room. She exited her room a few minutes later and walked down the stairs with a newly donned hoodie. Elma walked past me a third time without words at the bottom of the stairs, and I stared at her with burning anger in my eyes. Elma grabbed a bag from the dining room and stared at me from the across the room.

I said, "You did not say hi to me at all since I let you in. What did I do to you?"

She glared at me and said, "Your mother wants me to leave. I'm leaving. I can't do this shit anymore."

I quickly responded, "Okay. I understand, but did I do something to make you want to leave me?"

She stared at me in anger, and reiterated, "I told you I am not doing this shit anymore. Everyone is this house is sick in the head and I'm not going to deal with it."

I stared at Elma again, as I was taken aback by her general statement of the house's sickness in the head. She included me in that, and I couldn't believe she would say something so hurtful to me. Elma remained silent as she stormed past me with her belongings and out of the front door. She got into Stephanie's car, and I watched her leave the house one last time. Within minutes, my early morning went from watching cartoons in solitude, to me having an uncanny moment with Elma as she reappeared and disappeared out of my life.

My heart was heavy, because Elma made the choice to move out of the house and leave me in the lost direction of this home. I was also concerned about her physical and mental health onward. I turned the TV off and went outside to the front porch to sit down on the steps. It was cold outside, but the sweater I had on would suffice to keep me warm. I pulled the bottom of my sweater down as much as I could to create a barrier between my butt and the porch steps. I saw my breath as I exhaled and looked up at the sun shining that winter morning. Although my sweater kept me warm, I was completely numb by the absence of Elma. Within my racing thoughts, I replayed every interaction that I had with Elma from the moment she walked into our West End home, until those few moments ago, when she walked away. At the time, I was not certain if I'd ever see her again, but I truly felt the energy of her departure piercing through my abdomen and spine. The emotions and energy fluttering through the morning could not have been a stouter message to me that Elma departed from this household forever.

The energy in my heart felt desolate, and my body felt physically cold. I realized that I was still outside, and there were no shoes on my feet. In my thoughts through clairaudience, I heard my father say, *you still have to pay attention to what's around you when you daydream like that. You are freezing your tail off, go inside!*

I smiled and went inside.

A few weeks went by, and I started to notice Mother's behavior change. Like before, Mother was remaining in her room for much of the time when she was home. However, I noticed that she began to leave the door cracked open. It was clear that something was happening in Mother's mind, due to her inattentiveness to the habits I was used to. Because of this timeframe, I discovered that she was smoking cigarettes in the room while sitting on the bed and watching TV. I kept my bedroom door open because I wanted to listen to what Mother would do in her room now that Elma wasn't around. Mother seemed unmotivated by life, with an intense loneliness in her spirit.

One morning during the weekend, I noticed that she did not leave early to run errands. It was around ten a.m., and I made breakfast for Anne and myself. There were leftover eggs and pancakes for my mother, so I decided to bring her a plate to eat something.

As I opened the door to her bedroom, I heard her answer the phone and say, "Hi Stephanie, what's going on?"

Mother looked at me and smiled when I handed her the plate of food and stared down into the plate as she listened to Stephanie speak. Mother asked Stephanie to keep her updated with Elma's health and to call her if she needs anything.

She hung up the phone and looked up to see me standing next to her. Mother said, "Elma is not doing well. She has pneumonia now. It started with meningitis incidents, and now she has fucking pneumonia."

I said, "Oh. Ah, what is pneumonia?"

And Mother said, "It's when someone has trouble breathing because there is fluid in their lungs." She quickly dismissed me and asked me to leave her room.

I looked back as I exited the room and Mother picked up the fork to start eating her breakfast in distress. I was filled with worry, since Elma has been sick more than anyone around me in a matter of a year's time.

The following days turned into weeks in which Elma was in the hospital. I eavesdropped closely on Mother's phone calls between her and Elma's friend Stephanie in hopes of hearing progress of her health. I thought about Elma from the moment I woke up in the morning until I fell asleep at the end of each day. As I went through the days at school, playing outside with my friends to keep busy and finding food in the kitchen cabinets at night, I yearned for Mother to update me with how she was doing. I put my best effort forward to wake up as early as Mother did in order to engage in conversation with her during her best state of mind. There wasn't an alarm clock in my bedroom, since I naturally woke up at sunrise or when Elma was here, she used to wake me up.

The weeks progressed. Mother came home one rainy day. I was in my bedroom, and the grimness in her spirit irradiated through the house from the moment she walked through the foyer. Mother's energy made it evident that something had changed in Elma's health, which made me walk to the top of the stairs to meet Mother as she made her way upstairs. Mother was looking down at the stairs and did not notice me at first, and she forcibly smiled when she saw me at the top of the stairs. I followed her into the bedroom as she placed her work bag onto the bed and took her shoes off. Mother got undressed to change into her pajamas, and she said, "I just found out today that Elma slipped into a coma."

In my third eye, my inner viewing window displayed images from the scene in *The Matrix* movie where several corpses were encapsulated in a strange facility where the main character Neo woke up. I looked at Mother and said, "That doesn't sound good. What is a coma, something like when you are sleeping in a capsule?"

Mother sat on the bed and widened her eyes in bewilderment. She said, "Yes, it's something like that. How did you know that?" I looked away in misperception of her questioning me, in fear that she may be looking for a certain response from me. Although I was unsure, I expressed to her exactly what came to mind by saying, "The images popped in my head from the scene I saw when I watched *The Matrix*."

She reacted by tilting her head clockwise, and said, "When did you watch *The Matrix*?"

I responded, "I watched it downstairs with everyone one day when it was raining, and we couldn't play outside."

She nodded, and continued, "Oh okay. Well, let's hope she makes it out of this. But I'll let you know if I hear anything from Stephanie. As of now, it's not looking good." She shrugged and walked towards the other side of the room to grab her cigarettes.

I went to my room and told Anne the news about Elma. She stopped playing with her Hot Wheels™ and looked me in the face. She said, "Oh, that sucks." Anne turned around and reoccupied herself with playing with her toys.

I snapped back, "Do you not care that she's in a coma, or if she wakes up?"

Unfazed by my concerns, she continued to look down as she responded, "Elma is crazy, and she's been acting like a psychopath lately. I really don't care."

I lowered my eyebrows as I stared at her in disappointment and walked out of the room. I grabbed the purple Walkman from under my bed and double-checked the back for batteries. On the floor, there were tapes from R&B artists Aaliyah, Mariah Carey, Salt-N-Pepa, and Boyz II Men. I chose the Mariah Carey album and inserted the cassette tape into the Walkman. I anxiously exited my room and went to the front porch to listen to my Walkman in peace. I listened to the *Music Box* album and zoned out into the trees across the street on my neighbor's lawn. Elma left behind the Walkman that I was using, and I assumed that she must have forgot about it when she came to get the rest of her belongings a few weeks prior.

Clearly, there was some sort of shift happening. I did not understand what that "something" was, though I knew that nothing was in my control, but I was able to think through the circumstances that may come forth. As I sat on the porch, I smiled and thanked Elma aloud for the Walkman. The memories of her played through my mind, from the ugly to the beautiful. From the laughter to the anger, I saw in her eyes when she saw me under Chris's bed. I mentally hugged her in gratefulness that she saved me from what I believed would be an eternity of constant molestation under Chris's care.

Within days of Mother notifying me that Elma slipped into a coma, she returned to closing herself in her room immediately upon returning home from work. As time continued to pass, I made multiple attempts to ask Mother for updates on Elma in the early morning or in the late afternoon, whenever I could catch her. The update remained the same, in that she was in a coma.

To make matters worse, Mother started to date the gentleman, Chad, that she met at Morella's house a year or so earlier. Mother started to have Chad come over and visit the house. I noticed that Mother encouraged Anne and me to hang with Morella to use us as an excuse to additionally invite her mother Liona and Chad to the house.

The season started to change, and it was closing in on three months that Elma had been in a coma. Mentally, I prepared myself for Elma to never return. Even if Elma did recover from the coma and return, there was the possibility that Mother would remain upset with her since their last confrontation. I was unsure of the unknown future ahead, but I was not anticipating that things would go back to normal. At the time, I defined normal as Elma living in the house in decent health, confident that she cared about my wellbeing and safety.

On Easter morning, I woke up early in hopes that Mother would like to go to church for mass, since she had been depressed about Elma not doing well. One of my favorite holidays was Easter because I enjoyed wearing a poufy dress and twirling around in it. Typically, we did not have Easter baskets, participate in egg hunts, or anything like that unless we visited someone's house for the holiday. I really wanted to attend mass that morning because I figured that we needed to go and listen to the positive words spoken from Father Peter about the Bible. It was years since we attended church, but I was hopeful to go for Easter morning.

Instead, I woke up to solitude and silence throughout the household. I walked around quietly and kept myself busy by grooming my Barbie dolls and coloring. As the morning progressed, I went downstairs to eat a bowl of cereal for breakfast. As I sat at the kitchen table, I looked around the room and focused on the calendar on the wall. Today was Sunday, Easter morning. It also happened to be Elma's birthday. My eyes widened when I realized what day it was, and I felt a sharp transient pain in my stomach. It was my intuition speaking to me. I did not hear anything, and I did not see anyone or any images afterward. So, I started eating my bowl of cereal as I thought about what the plans could be for today once the house awoke.

I went upstairs to my bedroom and quietly entertained myself until others in the household awoke. Hours passed, and I toggled between watching a *Rugrats* marathon on Nickelodeon and going upstairs to play in my room. My sisters started to wake up around noontime, and Chris and Mother awoke shortly after. When Mother left her room to use the restroom, I followed her into the bathroom to say hello. She stared at the floor and ignored me. I rolled my eyes and went to my bedroom again. My twin stared at me but said nothing.

The doorbell rang, and I watched my mother walk down the stairs in her pajamas to see who the visitor was. I stood at the top of the stairs, peeking from the edge because I was being nosy, but I did not want Mother to see me. The person at the door was Stephanie, and she was wearing a peacoat with a dark blue fedora and sunglasses. When Mother opened the door, Stephanie gloomily locked eyes with my mother, took off her fedora, and placed the fedora to her chest. Mother immediately started to cry and embraced her in comfort. I watched Stephanie accept her embrace as the thought of Elma came to mind. I instantly knew that she was gone.

When Mother stopped hugging Stephanie, she thanked her for notifying her that Elma has passed away. Stephanie may have called Mother beforehand to confirm what was happening because she showed up without saying a word and left shortly after. Mother walked up the stairs and coldly said, "Elma passed away. She's no longer here."

She went to her room, and my twin and I immediately followed her. We sat on the bed with Mother, and Giovanna walked in. Mother then said, "Elma was in a coma, and it was decided by her siblings to unplug her from life support on her birthday today. They unplugged her at the time she was born. So fucked up, right?"

I widened my eyes in disbelief and frustration.

A million things came into my head and I started questioning every aspect of the future in my thoughts. I looked at the mirror in the direction of where Elma's stuff used to be in Mother's bedroom and said, "Well, what am I going to do now? Who is going to help me with my hair? Who is going to teach me new things to cook?" I realized that I just said this in front of Mother and in the presence of my sisters in the room. There was a slight sense of shame after I said that, and I continued to stare into the mirror in Mother's room. Tears rolled down my cheeks as I came to the realization that I will never see Elma's face again. Everyone was quiet as we were gathered in Mother's room, and I broke the silence by walking out abruptly. There was so much emotion stirring within me, and I needed solitude to think about the news I just received. Here I was, a nine-year-old girl lost in translation in between being a kid and trying to survive, mourning the loss of the second parental figure in my life.

In my room, I changed my clothes into something that I could get dirty in and ventured to the backyard to sit by the creek in solitude. As I stared down into the water trickling in between the pebbles along the stream, I started to relax my shoulders and loosen the tension in my face. My body, mind, and energy slipped away from me as tears began rolling down my face again. I felt defeated, especially since Elma, one of my protectors, was no longer with me. Elma will never return to live in the house with us again. We also could not mend our relationship from the last interaction, an argument we had a few months prior. My heart was hurting as I thought about Kenneth's death and his limited guidance whenever I could envision him in the form of spirit. I wondered if I would see Elma that way or if she was going to visit me. The thought of what the purpose of my life meant crossed my mind, and I thought about how long it would be until I was old enough to be on my own. The thought of life in the house without Elma frightened me, especially since I looked up to her insight and guidance. My mind was numb, and every thought in my head brought me back to the reality that she was gone. I went back into the house after sitting by the creek for a few hours. I cried all night in my bunk bed, feeling lonesome, with the notion that no one cared as much as I did about her passing.

I am extremely thankful for what Elma has shown and taught me, but I also am thankful for the things that I will never un-see in terms of her manic behavior towards the end. I was unable to understand who Elma was fully and get to know her better. Honestly, I did not care to understand. I loved Elma for who she was to me in the years I had her motherhood and direction when Mother was not emotionally there to provide for me. I thank Elma for stepping up when Mother was emotionally distraught from losing Kenneth. Elma taught me that stepping up to do the right thing did not have to be complicated, as Mother made it appear. Elma utilized her last years of life to care for us children while balancing the needs of Mother, as she taught me important things to be self-sufficient. In reflection, I somewhat believed that Elma knew that her time alive was transient after we met, and she wanted to make the best out of her last years to be there for us.

The following day when Mother arrived home from work, I asked her when Elma's funeral was and if she knew how her son Bobby was taking everything.

As she placed her bags down on her bedroom floor and continued to get undressed into her pajamas, she sharply said, "Elma's getting cremated. Her family is taking her ashes. I don't know how Bobby is doing." I thought about him, in hopes that he was okay. I did not see him again until he and I were adults.

Confused, I asked her what the word *cremated* means. Mother said, "It's when they burn your body into nothing but ashes. She's not having a funeral or getting buried in a cemetery like your father."

I felt pressure in my face as I tried not to cry again, and I responded to her, "So we will never see Elma again? Ever?"

And she said, "No."

Chris and Giovanna walked into the room, and I stared at Chris in disgust. Mother turned to them and unashamedly said, "Yeah, I just found out that Elma had AIDS, and that's what caused all of her issues towards the end. She didn't tell me she had fucking AIDS, and now I need to get tested."

I frowned in reaction to Mother's negativity towards whatever AIDS was, and I asked her to explain. She said, "It is an autoimmune disease where your body attacks itself. The disease can get passed on to another person."

I tilted my head in concern, and responded, "Does that mean that I could have it? I shared drinks and food with her. I used to wear her hoodies, could I have AIDS?"

She looked away to locate a cigarette and said, "No, AIDS is only contractable through contacting her blood directly through sex and needles."

Giovanna sarcastically replied, "Did you two ever touch each other's blood, like blood brothers? Are you two blood sisters and we don't know about it?"

I glared at her and said, "What is that, blood brothers?"

She scornfully said, "It's obviously when two people are bleeding from a fingertip and then touch each other to exchange and connect blood."

I looked at her in disgust and rolled my eyes. I left the room, because the energy in the room felt unmatched with my feelings of my world turned upside down and shaken up.

I thought about Mother's words in how she explained that AIDS attacked her body, so much that it facilitated pneumonia. Never have I heard of an illness that exists in which someone's immune cells can attack their own body. It sounded so foreign to me, since I was unaware of illnesses such as the common cold, chicken pox, and the flu. I wondered if Mother honestly knew that Elma had AIDS throughout her time here, but it didn't seem as though she did.

My mother and I got tested, and we were both negative.

Life After Elma's Peaceful Exit

It was springtime and I was nine years of age, working to navigate life after Elma's passing. I was determined to power through the remainder of the school year with as much mental strength as possible. It felt like a bad dream to come home with Elma in my mind, knowing that she was no longer alive. I found myself reaching for items such as the Walkman and a hoodie that she left behind to remember the support I felt from her. One day I was listening to her Walkman that she left behind with tears in my eyes, and Anne said to me, "Why are you even sad? Elma used to beat us, and she wasn't even our mother. How could you miss someone that hit us but wasn't our mother? I don't get it."

I was so taken back by her emotionlessness towards Elma that I frowned at her. I said to Anne, "Shut up. At least she cared about us and showed us how to do things. Mom never did that."

My twin ignored my response and walked out of the room. Her reaction gave me the notion that she did not want to see me upset about Elma's passing. She wanted me to move on.

In the house, in terms of supporting friends, Eric started to come around more since he knew about Elma's passing. I was thankful that Eric chose to come over again to be there for my twin and me, especially since Mother occupied herself with someone else. His friendship was Chris was still there somewhat after him finding out that he sexually abused us, because Eric chose us over Chris. Also, their relationship was not the same since Eric started dating Chris's ex-girlfriend Michelle during their break in friendship.

My friend Morella began to come over frequently with her mom Liona and their friend Chad. My friends Alana and Caroline would come over in addition to Morella to play with us and our neighbors outside. It started to be a routine where our friends and Morella's mom and friends would come over to play at the same time.

Within a few weeks, Chad started to come over more frequently without Liona or their other friend Ernest. Chad got along with Eric but tolerated Chris's presence for the sake of spending time with Mother. The relationship between Mother and Another quickly commenced, and there was seemingly an intimate relationship unfolding. Within two or three months, Chad moved into our house, which was only a few months after Elma's passing.

Mother's regimen at home changed slightly after Chad moved in, but it did not necessarily improve. Mother still disappeared into her bedroom whenever she was home, except when friends came over. Whenever my friends were inside of the house, Mother would come out momentarily to say hello to the girls and then return to her room. She adored all my girlfriends and showered them with love upon arrival. Mother wanted to exemplify that she was a "cool" mom, and she was caring and available to all. With Chad around, Mother began to have the new friends through him come over to the house whenever they were available. In conjunction with our friends in the house, Mother and friends would hang out in the common area with us as they drank dark-colored liquor, smoked cigarettes and weed, and played music. Of the friends through Chad, I liked Ernest because he had one blue eye, which was cool-looking, but more so because he always respected my twin and I. Ernest did not act strangely like Chris, but rather in the same way as Eric: he was interested in whatever we liked to do and how that was going for us. On a more confirmatory note of Chris's wrongdoings, seeing more men in the house like Ernest and Chad, in addition to Eric and Alana's brothers, showed me that my brother's behavior was not normal.

The summer following Elma's death and Chad's arrival was certainly a time of adjustments, in that my life quickly intertwined with Chad's family and my Mother through the two of them falling in love. I cannot confirm that Elma and Mother were together romantically in the timeframe in which Elma was in our house, but I did not see between them the same spur of infatuation stemming from Mother and Chad. She was completely smitten to be in a relationship with this man, which to me seemed like he was the company she wanted: people who wanted to party. With Chad and Mother partying a lot, they dragged us girls along with them to go see his family. Throughout the summer following, we attended multiple cookouts and parties in relation to Chad's family and friends.

Whenever we were stationed at our house, music was usually blaring more frequently than when Elma was around, whether we had company in the house or whether Mother was locked up in her bedroom. With Chad around, we were quickly introduced to the rap and hip-hop genres of music that was explicit to my virgin ears. I enjoyed the rawness of the music we were listening to, for example Ludacris and Nelly, because of the newness and ways in which music can be created. I was only aware of the R&B genre, and music that I termed "MTV music," which was mainly comprised of groups like the Backstreet Boys, NSYNC, Britney Spears, and Christina Aguilera. As new music genres were brought forth in the house with his presence, the only time that R&B music bled through the speakers was whenever I could blast music.

Chad's personality was generally quiet, and he often grunted instead of saying "yes" or "no" in response to anyone speaking to him. Chad reminded me of a teddy bear in human form because he was gentle in character, tall, heavyset, and had a dark skin complexion. In the first few months, a few times I caught Chad looking at Mother and blushing in fascination of his new girlfriend. It was nice to see someone new around her, I guess. My focus was that she was not spending time with us being an interactive mother, but rather dragging us places and letting us interact with others to keep us busy. Mother followed her same act in making us feel uncomfortable by making comments about how she makes good babies or how beautiful we were while squeezing our cheeks and mussing our faces. It was annoyingly inaccurate as to how we were treated, and it continued with Chad coming around. Throughout the summer going into the fifth grade, we ate so much food, and Mother often packed plates home for us to eat for several days afterward.

There was so much food to go around from the places we went, I started to notice both Mother and Chad packing on the weight. Luckily, Anne and I did not see this change.

The sibling energy between Chris and Giovanna and my twin and I was everchanging and distant. Around this time, Chris was completely entertained by Eric and Chad's new presence, which resulted in Giovanna hanging out with Anne and me more. Chris hung out with Eric and never attended gatherings at Chad's friends and family events, but we were not sure why. It was always us three girls, which on reflection I assume was due to Chad tolerating Chris's presence and inappropriate behavior that he was made aware of before he arrived. It was not long between the cookouts and parties that we three girls started to get our hair braided by Chad's nieces, into new styles such as cornrows and twists. From the moment that Chad's nieces began to braid my hair, I always reminisced on the moment that Elma voiced to my Mother her strong opinions about getting my hair permed. There is so much appreciation that I have in my soul for Elma on enforcing this on my Mother. The memory will never leave me that Mother tried to seek the easy way out by getting my hair permed, but thankfully, Elma fought in the moment and taught me how to manage my hair fundamentally. The dynamics with the house were ever changing.

Circling back to the house energy and spiritual encounters, it is imperative to note that the presence of more guests, such as Chad and Mother's new friends, did not halt the unnerving events. One example of this occurred when I was watching TV on the floor and Ernest was sitting across the room, near the kitchen on a folding chair. Everyone else was dispersed between the common areas and outside, but I specifically remember Ernest freaking out for a moment. As I sat there, I heard him say, "Oh hold up, what the hell is that?" I turned around to see him looking to his right, towards the kitchen.

He then said to me, "Carla, you didn't tell me there was no spirits in this damn house. There's a huge black figure in the kitchen doorway, and it's not moving!"

I looked at him and lowered my brows in worry while I cautiously approached the area near Ernest so I could see the spirit, too. I looked to my left, into the doorway, and there it was. I stared at the black figure in the doorway as Ernest stood up and said, "I got to get up out of here, are you coming outside with me?"

It was frightening because the black figure did not attempt to hide its appearance and continued to stand firm in the kitchen doorway.

Ernest walked outside through the front door and said, "There's ghosts up in there and today is not my day. I'm not going back inside."

Eric was coming in the front door and noticed the figure disappear as he entered the house. He stared at me and said, "Oh my God, was that it? Was that really what I thought it was?"

In distress, I nodded in response to the question. I knew that whenever I saw the black figure potently roaming the house or hovering in the corner of the room, it was guaranteed that the dreams I had that evening or the spirits I interacted with throughout the night would be terrifying.

Overall, it was safe to say that the summer was a time of change and different routines of each member of the household, including our newest member, Chad. Although my mind and spirit were still coping with the loss of Elma, one of my protectors, my healing process forced me to perceive Mother based on my life thus far. Within my nine years of existence on this Earth, I had already experienced the second reaction in Mother's behavior after the death of someone who was living with her. Moreover, both Kenneth and Elma were sleeping in the same bed as her and looking after her kids. To me, there was a pattern in the emotionless way she carried herself after the death of a loved one, and it unquestionably inscribed her level of selfishness towards us. There was a level of uncertainty in her desire for us, her children, to be around, and I felt that the bond between us, especially Anne and I, would remain cloudy until she showed empathy and love otherwise.

September 2001

I entered the fifth grade at East End Elementary School with excitement to finish our last year alongside my friends. It was cool to be in the top grade, because the younger kids treated us like the leaders of the school. Eric expressed to me that being a fifth grader was like being a younger version of seniors in high school and that it is a cool year to be in school.

When Anne and I arrived at school on the first day, I noticed that Alana was standing in the same line that Anne needed to be in for her class. Anne waved at me to signal that she was going to head over to the line with Alana. As she and my twin were waiting to enter the school building in their respective classroom line, I continued to walk to the back of the school, in sight of Alana's brother Alfred playing wallball. I noticed that Alfred was playing wallball with a few others, including an unfamiliar boy. The unfamiliar boy looked a little shy, yet his energy felt magnetizing to me, and for the first time, I was in awe of his presence. This was the first time I felt an attraction toward someone.

He had a very dark skin complexion, and his skin was silky smooth as if he was a model. However, as he played wallball with Alfred, his face looked serious, and he did not seem approachable.

Not knowing what to say to get the boy's attention, I walked up to Alfred and asked if I can play wallball with everyone.

He said, "Yeah, of course."

I made my way into the small crowd playing on the side of the school. Purposefully, I walked toward the boy I was newly attracted to and introduced myself. I said, "Hello, I'm Carla. What's your name?"

He looked at me and did not respond to my introduction.

I asked him, "What's the problem, I am just trying to say hello. Why are you ignoring me, hello?" He stared at me and mumbled something under his breath. Then, the boy punched me square in the face.

Absolutely in shock, I stared at him and shrieked, "What's your problem, why did you punch me?!"

Alfred started laughing in nervousness, and Alana came running toward me. She said," Oh my God, are you okay?" She then followed Alfred's lead and laughed.

I looked at her angrily and said, "I'm fine." I stared at her in disbelief that she was laughing, but then Alana explained that she tends to laugh when she got nervous. She looked towards Alfred and the boy and said, "It's not okay with Rob punching her in the face, though. What's wrong with you?!"

I looked at her and said, "So, you knew his name, but he couldn't say that his name was Rob? Why did I deserve that?"

Alfred looked at me and said, "Maybe you talk too much, and he didn't want to deal with you." And he walked away.

I lowered my eyebrows as Alfred walked to his line and noticed that Alana started yelling at Rob in my peripheral eyesight. I turned to her to see her shoving Rob.

Rob shoved Alana back, and she slapped him clear across his face in response. Alfred immediately proceeded toward Rob. In reaction to Alana slapping him, Rob just stared at her.

Rob looked at me as Alana shouted, "You never hit a girl, you hear me? The fuck is wrong with you?"

Rob walked past us and proceeded to walk away toward the classroom line, which happened to be the same as mine. In frustration and embarrassment, I walked up to my twin to engage in conversation in hopes that those who saw what happened would refocus their thoughts on the first day of school.

As the students entered school and into the hallway, I noticed that my twin and I were in classrooms adjacent from one another, and she had class with Alana, Caroline, and Morella. I quickly became friends with others in my classroom who were familiar faces from previous years in the school, in addition to the few that I already knew. Erica and Jessica were the two other girls that I knew, but our assigned seats slightly separated us throughout the classroom.

My assigned seat was next to the kid who just punched me, Rob Garrett. I felt an energy shift in my stomach as I started to station my belongings at my new desk. We were directly in front of the teacher, Mr. Guston, which was nice to know that anything Rob did could and would be seen by the teacher. Unfazed that I sat next to a newly found attractive boy who just punched me, I killed Rob with kindness for him to understand his wrongdoings.

Within a few days of forced interaction in class, he passed me a piece of paper with a note. It read, "I am sorry, I was wrong for hitting you. I am not a morning person and I did not react well to your high energy. You have a good friend who protected you. I'm sorry."

I stared at the note and felt the sincerity in his penciled words on the paper. When Mr. Guston faced the chalkboard to write class notes, I wrote back in response to his apology. It read, "Okay, but you're not just saying sorry because you sit here, right?"

Rob wrote, "No. It's because you are nice, and I am not used to that. I am from Newark and was told to never trust nice people because they usually want something in exchange for their kindness."

I read the note and stared at him before writing back. My response read, "You should judge for yourself if the person is worth trusting. You will know that by how you feel." I slid the paper to him, then focused on my classroom work.

About a week into the school year, we were sitting in class when Mr. Guston received a phone call from the principal's office. I remember his face was very solemn, and he then widened his eyes in disbelief on what he was hearing. He hung up and then said to everyone, "A plane crashed into the World Trade Center, and the building is on fire. I need to turn on the television. Jennifer and Jessica, please go to the principal's office, your guardians are here to remove you from school."

Everyone started to chatter and panic, but I stared at Jessica as she waved bye to everyone and exited the classroom. I did not understand what the World Trade Center was, but I listened to everyone chatter in trying to make sense of what was happening. Finally, someone else in the class asked the question burning in my mind, "What is the World Trade Center?"

My teacher then said, "For those of you that do not know what the World Trade Center is, it's the building known as one of the Twin Towers located in New York City." He continued, "I suggest we keep vigilant of the windows and wait for direction from the principal. Everyone needs to stay calm, and we will try our best to continue with the day."

Within minutes, Mr. Guston received multiple calls from the principal's office to send children downstairs to go home with their caretakers. As people were leaving the classroom, I noticed that Rob and I were two of the few kids remaining in the classroom, which was half full since the news that morning.

Before lunchtime, Mother came in to pull us out of school. I met Anne in the hallway where we stared at each other in disbelief that Mother called us out of school. In unison, we walked downstairs to the principal's office. Mother appeared to be in a state of manic worry, but also happy that we were leaving with her. Confused that Mother was acting concerned in front of the secretary and other faculty members, she ushered us to the car in silence. When we were in the car and securely pulling out of the school parking lot, I unashamedly asked her why she pulled us out of school. There was a moment of silence as she drove scarily fast from the moment we got onto Route 22 east, towards northern New Jersey.

Moments before Mother responded, my inner window appeared in front of my vision to bring forward images of Mother's friend Chris. In this image, he was standing in a parking lot in his firefighter gear. I was not sure what it meant, but my image would be clarified soon after.

After a long pause, Mother responded to my initial question by saying, "We are going to Liberty State Park to see Chris before he goes to New York City with the fire truck. They ordered for their fire department over there to assist with the Twin Tower buildings."

As I anticipated asking her why we were going with her to see Chris, she continued, "Chris is your biological father. Kenneth did not want either of you to ever meet him, but since he's no longer here with us, I wanted you to meet Chris and have a relationship with him. I had to build up the relationship a little before telling you; it was only fair. I'm sure you figured it out by now, but he's your real father. We are going to see him and give him a hug for good luck. He may not make it back."

I stared at her facial expression from the backseat, looking through the rearview mirror. As expected, Mother's facial expression did not display much of a reaction. I didn't know which part of this situation I should be more annoyed with, her terrible driving all the way to our destination or the lack of emotion towards the fact that she officially communicated the news that Chris was our biological father.

We arrived at a park where we could see the New York City skyline in proximity. I had never been here before, and to me it was powerful to experience the building on fire so close, yet so devastating. Before I could ask Mother what park we were at, we drove past a sign that read, "Liberty State Park." When we arrived, he was standing outside of the firetruck walking towards the car. There was a feeling of anxiousness extruding from Chris' energy as we arrived, and I remember getting out of the car quickly to hug him and say good luck.

The other firefighters were in the truck and looked on as he said to us, "Hi honeys, I drive the truck, so they couldn't tell me that I can't make a stop. I have to go now, but I wanted to give my babies a hug before I left." He smiled and looked at Mother.

She said, "They know."

He looked at me and nodded. We hugged, and he turned to the truck to get on the road again. We sat there as we watched him drive away, but we also looked outward, as we saw the Twin Tower buildings in disarray. We could hear the fire trucks, the yelling, and the commotion of the world in New York City from the other side of the river. Mother demanded we get back in the car to leave immediately, and we drove home quickly through side roads and other unknown highways to beat the traffic and other cars trying to get away from the city.

Throughout the car ride, I thought about what the burning buildings meant to everyone in the world, not just the people of New Jersey and New York. I thought about my newly revealed father's safety and wellbeing. More than anything, I reasoned through why

Kenneth did not want us to see my father while he was alive, and why he may have taken his life. I circled back to thoughts of Elma and stared out the window as the thought of gaining and losing people seemed to be normal yet heart-wrenching.

We arrived home, and I put my belongings into my room. Mother turned on the television in her bedroom and I walked in since she left the door open. I adjusted my focus to the news on television and live updates on the Twin Towers, with my thoughts overflooding with grief. A whirlwind of emotions sifted through my body as my mind raced about the world. From within my own journey and as a whole entity, the world was hurting in this moment. Tears filled my eyes in frustration, feeling emotionally tired from the rollercoaster year.

I lost Elma in the beginning of the year, the world lost the singer Aaliyah a few weeks prior, and now we were sorting through today's event of the Twin Towers burning on live television. In this moment, my heart ricocheted with feelings of pain protruding from the world around me, my spirit, and fear of the unknown ahead. I was unaware of the significance of the Twin Towers in terms of business, radio, and other financial companies ... but I was aware that this was a major hit to the world through my connection of the energy from the television in Mother's bedroom. I cried for hours as I stared at the screen.

Antics with Chad's Company

Even though the addition of Chad has brought new friends around to establish familial friendships within our household, there were situations that arose, that made me wonder if his presence was beneficial to Mother or a hindrance. Shortly after Chad's arrival and adjusting heavily to the summer of partying with his family and friends, Chad's brother Dave, Dave's wife, and their five children became homeless. Although I was unsure of their living situation and why the house was no longer habitable for the seven of them, Mother offered to let them to move into our house. Keep in mind, we were a house of six people.

I found out the news when I was eavesdropping from the top of the stairs on a conversation between Mother, Chad, and Dave in the living room. As Mother proceeded up the stairs and saw me standing at the top, she said, "Go upstairs and make some room in your drawers. Move your stuff around so that you can fit one of the girls in the room with you and Anne."

I hurriedly turned around and entered my room. I told Anne that we needed to consolidate our drawers immediately to let one of Dave's daughters stay in our room. Giovanna overheard me tell Anne and asked me what was happening. I told her that Mother instructed us to make room for them because they were going to stay here, and she angrily went downstairs to confront Mother. Mother was indifferent, and she instructed us to make way for people moving in.

Of the five siblings, two of them were females and there were three males. One of the boys was my age, the other one was younger, and the oldest one was around Giovanna's age. The two girls were older than Giovanna and Chris, but they were close in age. Either way, within hours of the conversation held in the living room, Chad's brother's family was moved into our house.

Chris did not have to move his belongings around for any of the seven people moving in, which I assume was because of his past and Chad's uncertainty of trust in his behavior. I believe Chad was aware of what occurred with Chris's molestation, especially since he confided with Eric for companionship more than Chris. Dave, his wife, and the boys lived throughout the common area of the downstairs. Even though we did get along with the seven of them, we only knew them in the state in which we visited their house a few months ago, when the summer started. Moving forward, I will refer to Chad's brother and family as the Garrettsons for simplicity.

The Garrettsons never attended the same school as us and continued to attend school a town over. They either rode bicycles or hitched a ride with Dave when he felt like driving them to school. Dave's wife, Diamond, cooked dinner, but it was mostly Southern soul food, which is a comfort food to consume in moderation. Although I did not see the effects of the delicious but unhealthy soul food at the time, Mother and Chad gained weight on a weekly basis, and I was concerned for their health. I joked around behind closed doors and called Mother Miss Piggy from the *Muppets*, but both Mother and Chad exceeded 400 pounds each. Alongside my twin and I, the Garrettsons did not gain weight.

The boys in the house were respectful to me by not trying to do anything physically, but I sensed that the brothers were attracted to the three of us girls. Giovanna seemed to be spending a lot of time with the older girl that she shared a room with, and it seemed like they were dating. I did not know then that Giovanna liked girls, but it came across as such.

Chris completely ignored everyone in the house and spent a lot of his time with Eric and Chad, and now Dave. They started to drink dark liquor daily, which I soon learned was cognac, and would get drunk throughout the week. They would play card games, smoke in the house, and play vulgar rap music. One day, Chad and the boys were so drunk that they opened our dining room door to walk out. This door was special because it exited the house as one would expect, but there was no porch, stairs, or anything to support the six-foot space between the door and the backyard grass. They followed one another as they drunkenly walked outside, to fall straight down into the backyard. As mentioned earlier, the yard was not well kept, and thus their landing into the backyard was like walking into a cornfield with no machete to see your way through. The drunkenness continued day in and day out, and Diamond and Mother drank with them, in addition to smoking something like that smelled like plastic burning.

With things rapidly changing in the past year or so after Elma's passing, the upkeep of changes brought forth with Chad's presence came. Especially since I used to go to my bedroom for privacy, I did not have privacy anymore with a "cousin" living in the room with us. During this time, Mother asked for us to not have people over in the house except for Eric. The exclusion of our friends, including Morella, meant we had to go outside if we wanted to hang out with friends. The worst part of the energy shift with new members in the house was the continuance of spiritual ordeals, as they never fell short in this household. The Garrettsons noticed as well, and they were freaked out to say the least. The energy stirring was brewing and got worse. It got so intense that a priest had to come in the house. I will mention this part in a little.

There were several instances in which one of the Garrettsons would approach one of us in concern about having an interaction with a spirit. One of the Garrettsons approached Giovanna about a spirit sitting next to them on the bed and pulling the sheets from them. Another time, one of the Garrettsons informed me that the couch was shaking when they were trying to sleep one night. One other time, one of them was sleeping and heard growling, as if there was a panther in the house. When he looked across the room, he met a pair of red eyes and a large black cat, resembling a panther growling at him. All in all, in addition to our experiences, the Garrettsons also noticed spiritual phenomena at the house, just as our friends who came over before had endured similar experiences with the spirits. The validity of each story cut deeper through any doubt that we lived in a haunted house.

The seven people who moved into our home certainly felt the difference after moving in, but we felt the pains of their presence, too. There was only one bathroom in our house, and multiple mouths to feed. Everyone was uncomfortable in the house, but Mother and Chad were unfazed because their space was not compromised by the presence of the Garrettsons. The brothers were arguing a lot over space in the common area. In the overall routine of things, it was chaotic to fight over the bathroom and fight over food in the kitchen. I talked to my neighbors, the Nobels, since they were familiar with living in a house with several siblings, and one of the girls gave me a good piece of advice. One day when we were playing outside, she said to me, "It's going to be okay, Carla—you'll get used to it. We alternate showering every other day. It just makes things easier. Try not to get too dirty on the first day, and if you need to, use a washcloth with soap to wipe yourself down in the bathroom sink. It's actually not good to shower every day because it's not good for the skin." I nodded, and thanked her for the tips.

In terms of the Garrettson girls, they continued to braid our hair once a week for the first month of living in the house. The girls were old enough to work and were able to find new jobs within a few weeks. When the two girls started working, they were in the house as little as possible. I started to notice that my costume jewelry such as my earrings and necklaces went missing piece by piece, and my piggy bank was emptied and placed back together to look untouched. Things were always disheveled in my room, as if someone was searching through my belongings every chance they could. Not only were the girls taking my stuff, but Giovanna was also having the same issues of items missing from her room, and she brought it to my attention.

Giovanna pitied their living situation and was sure to voice this when she told Mother about the missing items from our bedrooms. However, she also made it clear to Mother that she did not tolerate someone stealing from her, because this was never an issue before.

Mother did not want to confront Dave and Diamond about the issues we were having and left our concerns unaddressed. She valued Dave and Chad and their connection in having fun through the difficulties in their lives. Mother was well blinded by the masked depression from the tragic losses of two important people in her life, as it was evident to me that she preferred to put her internal traumas on the backburner.

The Garrettsons also brought a physical burden with them to the house as well. I began to see little bugs in the kitchen and an accumulation of them as time went by. It was not long until Eric was in the kitchen one day and yelled, "Holy shit, is that a roach?!"

I heard him from the other room, and I walked into the kitchen and said, "That's what they are, roaches? How did they get here?"

Eric indicated that the Garrettsons likely brought roaches into our home when they moved in because they weren't there before. It was a change that I had to get accustomed to, especially since they were multiplying. Roaches would come out of the cereal boxes that were not properly sealed when I poured by cereal in the morning, or in my pancake mix when I wanted to make pancakes. The worst moment was the day that I quickly grabbed water from the faucet after a day of playing outside and there was a roach in my cup. As I drank the water, I felt movement in my mouth and immediately saw the image of a roach in my inner window. I spit the water onto the kitchen floor, and the roach scurried away. My blood boiled, and I was through with the invasion of privacy in our home. Even with the new roach problem in the house, Mother went through her days unfazed and happily in love with Chad.

In school, I was excited about being a fifth grader and feeling on top of the world in our school. Rob and I slowly but surely got along because we were next to each other in class and were always chit-chatting. We continued to write notes to one another daily, and I started studying with him outside of school in the field, on the school steps, or on the pavement where we originally met in the back of the school. He lived two blocks from our school, and I saw him more since he hung out with Alana's brother Alfred often. Eventually, he asked me if I wanted to be his girlfriend one day after school. I stared at him, smiled, and said yes.

I befriended a girl who was in our class a few weeks into the school year when I observed our similar outgoing personalities in Mr. Guston's class. We never played during recess or spoke outside of the classroom until one morning I saw her getting picked on.

I was walking up the driveway at the front of the school to get into the classroom line, and I saw her yelling different phrases to multiple people like "Shut up!" "They are not fake!" and "Leave me alone!" almost in tears. She was flustered over others shouting slander about her breasts being fake as a fifth grader.

As I got closer, someone make a remark to her that they could not believe that her parents would pay for her to get a boob job at ten years old, and they should get in trouble for it.

She put her hands over her breasts and walked away from everyone.

I followed her, and I said, "Hey, are you okay? Don't let these people bring you down. They are so jealous that you're developed already! You have no control of that."

She looked at me and quickly said, "I did not want this, I had no control over how fast they are growing. I told my mother that I want them removed but she said that they may still grow. I'm so sad, Carla. I'm Donna by the way. I never introduced myself to you."

I looked at her, frowned, and said, "Don't be sad. I'll yell at whoever talks to you or tells you that your boobs are fake. That's messed up."

Alana and Caroline heard the commotion and walked towards Donna and I. Alana stood silent, but Caroline said, "Yeah. What Carla said. We don't think they are fake."

And the three of us hugged.

Alana smiled, but walked away in disinterest at the emotional interaction. I didn't understand why she was not sorry for Donna, but I mentally noted her emotionlessness towards Donna in that moment.

Throughout the school year, I filled my time with hanging outside of my house and spending the least amount of time with anyone in the household. I started hanging out more on Alana's block when she and I discovered a shortcut to walk through to her street that did not entail walking through the woods along the brook. The shortcut walk-through was an open patch of land between the houses on Delacy Ave. and Westervelt Ave.

Because of the cut-through, I quickly became friendly with the young couple that owned the house adjacent to the patch of land, which I assume was their grass. Anne and I would rake their yard during the fall and shovel their driveway in the winter. The other house that was adjacent to the other half of the grass was inhabited by an old man. He seemed neutral about us crossing through every day and would wave from his porch as we passed through. The other side, on Westervelt, there wasn't anyone living in the two houses when we discovered the cut-through because they were newly built. As we approached the summer, both houses on the became inhabited around the same time. We got in the habit of running through the second part of the cut-through because we did not know the neighbors and did not know if they were okay with us walking through their newly inhabited yards.

One day that summer, Alana, Anne, and I were walking across the cut-through, we were almost out of it when we saw one of the neighbors come out to his back porch of his newly built home on Westervelt. He was standing there in the backyard with a rifle and threatened us to not come back through his yard ever again. We knew that we weren't supposed to be trespassing, but we were just kids trying to save some time to play outside longer. We ran through his front yard and onto the street in Westervelt in fear of the neighbor, but laughed because he never came around the front. Although we knew he was just trying to spook us with a rifle, the man built a fence weeks later. We were forced to go around the entire block moving forward.

As springtime came around, Mother's weight was steadily increasing, and she was prescribed a breathing machine. She was diagnosed with sleep apnea by the doctor and always needed an inhaler with her. Mother was having trouble moving around the way that she used to, and her patience was running thin with the Garrettsons because of how much they did not respect the house. To me, the Garrettsons believed the house was an all-inclusive free hotel with full range of the house, excluding Chris's and Mother's room. In the moments when my Mother was not doing anything private in the bedroom, she would open the door for us to spend time with them since the energy in the house was shifting all over the place. Through a few instances of going to her room to see how she was doing, I learned a few things about her behavior and things that she was going through. Especially since the Garrettsons were occupying so much space, Mother allowed for us to convene in her room to make plans. The first thing I noticed was how Mother and Chad's facial expressions and energy levels drastically changed from the moment she arrived home and went into her room, to the time that she opened the door an hour or so later. Typically, their state went from calmness yet alertness in their eyes to looking drowsy and inattentive of the environment. Undoubtedly, it reconfirmed what I have perceived about her secret habits throughout the years with Elma being around and now Chad. They were not as good as hiding it, but they were doing something in the room in that time and she was not herself when she came out of the room. Frankly, I was not sure of what "being herself" meant because I did not know her well. However, something Mother was doing caused her to be under the influence, but I could not see what it was exactly. Sometimes the room was smoky when I entered and it smelled like burnt plastic, but sometimes it was not. I had no idea what it could be, so I continuously tried to move past it. I was content that Mother allowed for us to be in her room, anyway.

During this time, I also learned Mother was having issues with money management, and she was likely going to lose the house when she filed for bankruptcy. Since Kenneth's passing, she has accumulated many medical bills due to her weight gain and health issues, ranging from depression, sleep apnea, to newly acquired diabetes. Kenneth also wrote several fictitious checks in his last year of life in Mother's name to pay for a plethora of things, from groceries to auto bills. In turn, this caused her to go into collections with several companies due to her unawareness of the bill accruals. There was a place of sadness in my heart towards Mother when she angrily spoke about this, but that quickly changed when I asked her why Kenneth took his own life. The question came about because I could not believe that he would do that to her, and it made me wonder why he would do something like that. I did not understand Kenneth's motives and perception of his reality.

When I asked Mother if she knew why Kenneth took his life, Mother said that it was because of the existence of my twin and me.

Chad put his head down and walked out of the bedroom in anticipation of the conversation about to unfold.

Mother continued to explain that we were complete mistakes, and we should not have been born, and if she did not keep us, things would have been different. Her response startled my twin and me. Truthfully, it stopped me in my tracks, and made me realize that we were merely a nuisance of existence in her eyes. I quickly exited and went to my bedroom. I put on Elma's hoodie and made my way outside to the creek in the backyard. That comment Mother said never left me. Even though I have forgiven her for her mental instability, life would not be the same knowing she believes that my existence caused Kenneth's death.

As school rounded out into the final days of my elementary years at East End, Rob and I decided to be friends and not continue dating. It was a mutual decision, especially since we had the same circle of friends and would see one another frequently. Our relationship would remain as friends going into the intermediate school together.

On the last day of school, my twin and I were hovering in the classroom, waiting for our friend's mom to finish talking to the teacher for us to all go downstairs together. The friends were a pair of fraternal twins who Anne and I met in the first grade, a boy named Greg and a girl named Connie. Anne and I were hovering around with Alana waiting, and that's when we saw Connie and Greg's mother collapse to the floor in the classroom.

Alana yelled, "What just happened?!" and her teacher, Mr. Falcon, rushed us down the stairs and away from the scene while my teacher Mr. Guston tried to revive her.

Alana and I stayed outside in the parking lot to wait around for the twins, but we decided to leave when we saw the ambulance arrive and personnel rushing inside.

That day, Connie and Greg lost their mother. It was a shock to the community because of how their mother was a big part of the parent teacher association, and everyone knew her. I mention this story because the aftermath of this occurrence impacted their lives for many years to come. Their mother was everything to them and such a strong influence in their life.

For me, it was a time of mourning for them through the tragic loss of their mother, yet it brought me back to the day that I lost Elma. I cried for their loss of their mother, although I knew that their father would be there for years to come and support them through everything. As I cried, I wondered why the emotion of crying did not trigger thoughts of the day I could lose of my mother. As I walked home from school that day, a million thoughts went through my head as to why my mother was not first in my mind, and why she did not love and support me the way their mother did. It made me think about what was considered a normal relationship amongst a family, and what was not. The loss of their mother moment made me realize that the relational side of my family life teetered towards the abnormal. I was convinced that my family life was not functionally healthy.

Intermediate School

Of the other issues at hand in the household, Mother kicked the Garrettsons out of the house shortly after she came home from work and flipped the house upside down with her explosive energy. She took out her anger out on every single person, including Eric since he was present as the events unfolded. Everyone was highly uncomfortable because of the way she handled the situation. The older Garrettson girls moved out within days of the incident, and slowly but surely, they all left, one by one. They were all moved out by the summer, but we still had a roach problem.

On the other hand, Chris finished his senior year in high school and Mother encouraged him to join the military for discipline and stability in his life. Secretly, I was excited that he would possibly be out of the house in addition to the Garrettsons and away to start his own life in adulthood. I recall that he and Eric went downtown to the local military center to sign Chris up for the military. His acceptance into the military was speedy, and he was set to depart after he graduated high school.

During the summertime after the Garrettsons and Chris left the house, Mother received a letter in the mail and multiple phone calls about my twin and I to audition for a modeling gig, potentially to be in a commercial on TV. When Mother told us about it, I was so ecstatic because I loved to sing, and figured modeling may be a good way to get my foot in the door to have a singing career. Although I was unsure of how modeling could lead into becoming a singer, I knew that Mariah Carey had a traumatic childhood from what I saw on television, and she made it big in her music career. She made it through her mother's career, but I believed that modeling would help me get exposed to the right people. Based on my knowledge of her and highly recognized New Jerseyans such as Whitney Houston and Lauren Hill, I believed I could swing a singing career if I started early. Nonetheless, Mother wearily said that she will take us to the modeling agency in northern New Jersey, and we made our way there one Saturday morning for our appointment. On the car ride there, I recalled feeling surprised that she was active in taking the first step to go to the modeling agency, and this opportunity was happening.

We arrived at the modeling agency and we sat in the waiting room as Mother filled out some paperwork. As she stood at the counter, my inner window appeared. The memory of Mother yelling at the therapist the first day of us going to therapy for Chris's behavior came back to view. Initially, I was perplexed and mentally asked for an explanation of why the memory showed up. In Elma's voice, she swiftly said, *"Your mother is going to make a scene and you're not getting much farther than today. Don't count on it. Sorry."*

The inner window closed, and I looked over to Anne. She said, "What? What's wrong?"

And I said, "Nothing."

She stared at me and said, "What did you see? You saw that something was going to happen, and we wouldn't be able to do this shit."

I looked at her, nodded, and looked at the floor in anger.

After a few minutes, the agency representative called the three of us into a room and opened the portfolios that were initiated for each of us. As I sat there, I tried not to think of the image I was revealed in the waiting area, and I smiled as the representative asked Mother questions. The representative asked for more photos to be taken for the portfolio and for them to be taken in house, under their contract.

Mother asked the representative for clarity on the pricing, and they explained. Although I cannot recall the pricing, Mother was unhappy about the amount of money it would cost for us to get started under the agency's contracting. She asked the representative, "Why did you waste my time to drive an hour, for me to be told that there was an extensive amount of money involved?" The representative kept calm, but Mother made it clear that she was upset with the lack of communication upfront. We left abruptly, and as expected, Mother made a scene in the waiting room on her way out by telling everyone there that the agency was a scam.

We got in the car, and Mother said, "Yeah, there's no way you will be doing any of this if it's going to cost this much. Consider something else if you can't get something through school, because I'm not paying thousands of dollars for you two to model. Nope. That shit should be free!"

On the way home, I stared out of the window and towards the highway. The thought of her lack of sacrificing a little money now for something that could pay off eventually bothered me. If something did not directly benefit Mother, she was not interested. I thought of how she recently purchased expensive name-brand clothing like Coogi for herself and Chad, but still bought us Kmart shoes. Although money did not matter to me, especially since I did not know much about money, why was she so reluctant to spend money and invest in her family? At home, we did not have curtains, carpets, or much food to salvage through, yet she has expensive clothes and partied with her friends a lot. At that age, I understood that a career in singing or music takes time, based on what I have seen on television and hearing stories on the radio about artist come-ups. From Britney Spears in the Mickey Mouse Club to Destiny's Child as a group of girls singing from a young age, I knew that the time to start was now. Mother crushed that option for us and told us in several different ways throughout the car ride that we could do something else instead.

At home, Giovanna obtained her first job working at a pet store in town, and Chris was off to the military. Anne and I loved riding our bicycles to see Giovanna at the pet store so that we could play with the animals whenever she was not busy. Giovanna brought home a rabbit one day, followed by another one, followed by another one. Within a blink of an eye, we had an outdoor hutch with ten rabbits living in our backyard.

Eric came around less frequently to be with us or hang with Chad to have a drink or two. He also came by to help Mother by picking up her prescriptions, bringing us food, or whatever else she needed. As expected, Eric needed to live his own life and started to come by less often since he was working full-time and his relationship with Michelle, Chris's ex-girlfriend, was becoming long-term.

Anne and I kept busy to stay away from the house and let Mother live her life with Chad. We started coming home later and later into the evening, and no one batted an eye at us or cared about our whereabouts. We noticed that Chad was usually drunk watching television with Coca-Cola and dark liquor readily available nearby, but from time to time, Mother would be gone. She would then come home late, sometimes later than us, and lock herself in the room per the usual.

As Mother was in and out of the house, we quickly observed the dynamic in terms of meals, attention, and priorities having shifted for the wellbeing of everyone in the house. She stopped food shopping altogether, and thus Anne and I decided to break into the bedroom at night to steal her debit card. It was not hard to do this, especially since Mother slept with a breathing machine and Chad snored so loud. It became a weekly thing for us to do. We knew her pin number on her debit card by watching her put it in at the grocery store in the past, so we could access her cash.

When we broke into their room in the middle of the night, we would ride our bicycles to the bank on Somerset, and take at least 200 dollars, depending on her balance. From there, we would wait until the next day and go to Acme to buy groceries for us to cook pasta, rice, chicken, pork, and usually canned veggies. We knew how to sauté onion, tomato, and garlic, and cook veggies like corn and whatever else could be heated up in a can, but we did not master handling fresh greens like broccoli or asparagus. We never ate anything remotely good for the body in that time.

Since the dynamic was evidently changing yet again, there were more adjustments to be made in our routine and lifestyle. Anne and I did not want to intrude in Alana's house and ask for food because there were already five kids to feed. There was a 7-Eleven across the street from Alana's house, so we were able to use the money we "borrowed" from Mother to buy something to eat. Sometimes we stole from the 7-Eleven because it was easier that way, but I felt so guilty the first few times that I stopped soon after. The people who worked at the store were nice, and every time I would steal a bag of chips or a honey bun, my body burned up from the inside out because of the guilt. Due to the additional remarks Elma and Kenneth would make or the looks I got from them in my third eye, I knew I had to stop.

On the Fourth of July before entering the sixth grade, we were by Alana's house, and rallying up on our bicycles to get a head count. There were fifteen of us and we did not all have bikes, so we were sorting out who can jog it out to the West End of town, and who had pegs to allow someone to ride with them across town. Since we were going to see the fireworks, we were all on a mission to get there by sunset. Anyhow, I was on my bike doing circles in the street as I waited for everyone to get tallied, and out of nowhere I heard my friend Erica scream, "Carla, car!"

I looked to my right to see a car slamming on its brakes. The car was headed right towards me and was turning sideways in an attempt to not hit me on the bicycle. It still collided into me. Thankfully, the impact was low, since the side of the car hit me instead of its front. I was knocked off my bike onto the pavement. In addition to the car, I also decreased the effects of the impact by rolling when my body hit the street.

All my friends turned, in fear of the worst, but I heard one yell, "Oh thank God she's alive, I can't imagine losing Care-Bear!" I smiled because everyone was worried, but they knew I was okay. Care-Bear was my nickname coined by my friends, I am pretty sure Alana, because I reminded them of the *Care Bears* cartoon. The car that hit me quickly drove away when I got up from the pavement, and my friends tried to chase the woman. They were unsuccessful. I had scuffs on my knees, arms, and hands from the fall, but I continued with my evening. We watched the fireworks on the West End of town. No one in the house except Anne knew that I fell, and they did not notice the scuffs from the fall.

At some point in the summertime, Mother brought us to northern New Jersey once or twice to visit Chris, my recently confirmed biological father. Per usual, Chris was ecstatic to see us, but his demeanor has always been serene in his emotional approach. His simple smile was warm and inviting, yet his thoughts and energy were shooting in a million directions when he interacted with us. Now that we officially had established the meaning of his presence in our lives and the reason for the visits since the age of five after

Kenneth's passing, Chris was ready to tell us more about our family: his other children.

When I saw Chris that summer, he asked me, "What grade are you going into now, the sixth grade?"

I nodded.

He said, "Okay, well hold up. Let's talk about something. Now, you got a brother that's exactly your age who could pretty much be your triplet. His birthday is a day after yours, which makes you a day older than him. His name is Chris, too."

I stared at him and thought, "Wait a second, is he serious?"

And before I could respond, he said, "I'm serious, Carla. So, you have two brothers named Chris, and my name is Chris. But you should call him to say happy birthday. I'll let you talk to him on the phone, just have your mother call me." He looked at Mother for her confirmation, and she nodded.

Anne stared blankly at Chris as he continued explaining the other siblings we have, and how old they were. He looked at me and said, "Carla, you are my oldest daughter." And we finished our visit at the firehouse. On the ride home, I stared out of the window in disbelief and excitement that I had another brother our age. More than anything, I was curious about what my other siblings were like in comparison to the ones I resided with.

A few days before the first day of sixth grade, we received a letter in the mail regarding the updated location of where sixth-grade students would attend school. Since construction was still underway and the intermediate school building was not ready, the letter instructed students to go to the high school for attendance.

Anne and I were ready to go to school, yet nervous to be in a building with the older kids. It seemed like we were walking into a university campus with no direction, but Alana and the girls decided that we would walk with Alana's brothers to school together for the first day. The night before the first day of school, Mother instructed Anne and me to pack our bags because we were going on a road trip. We were so confused, because we knew that school started tomorrow, but she told us we were going on a trip instead.

The following morning, I watched Giovanna get ready for school as we packed Mother's car with our belongings for ten days' worth of clothing per her request. In confusion, I asked Mother why we weren't going to school and where we were going.

Without looking at me, she happily said, "We are taking a road trip down south. We are going to see Chad's family in Atlanta." I looked at Anne in excitement, as I almost forgot that Alana and our friends expected to walk to school with us that morning. I politely asked Giovanna to let Alana know that we went on a road trip with Mother so that she didn't wait for us, and she nodded.

We set out for Georgia. We stopped at South of the Border hotel between North and South Carolina to experience it and the area. As we arrived in Georgia, Mother happened to drive through Savannah as the sun was setting, and we enjoyed the beauty of a real sunset over the sight of the nearby Talmadge Bridge. The view of the bridge at sunset was an array of every color one would desire in a sunset, from yellow to crimson red, and bleeding into a deep purple. The view was gorgeous as Mother drove a different highway parallel to the bridge. Truly, for once in our lives, my twin and I felt like we were on a vacation. My twin and I had each other through the trip, and Chad and Mother enjoyed their time together as we allowed them. We kept each other entertained throughout the family visits and Native American museums that we visited in Georgia, and we loved the hot weather more than anything. As expected, the food was unforgettably delicious, and I fell in love with biscuits and gravy. The trip up and down the East Coast was not bad, since I brought a book to read and my atomic purple Game Boy Color with extra batteries.

Once Anne and I arrived home and walked to school the following morning with Alana, the school staff would not let us in the building because we missed the first week and a half. Although we had a schedule originally mailed to us, due to Mother's spontaneous vacation, the school removed us from the roster. From school, we called Mother's job to let her know that she needed to go with us to formally register us at school before we can attend.

Once we got into school, Anne and I started school in the high school building. It was absolutely frightening and overwhelming, to say the least. Truthfully, the diversity between the grade levels was complex, but the complexity continued into fear of the unknown due to the three elementary schools that merged into the intermediate-school level. From this, I quickly recognized some classmates from the other two schools I attended in kindergarten or saw during sports.

Luckily, we were able to reconnect with a few friends immediately as they remembered us. One of the friends that we recognized was Jayden, one of the kids who was the nicest to us in

Stony Brook and played with us during recess. He was extremely happy to see Anne and I again after several years and rekindled his friendship with us immediately. Anne and Jayden were together so much that they officially called one another boyfriend and girlfriend. Honestly, I was puzzled by this because Anne, based on my observations and the behaviors she had exhibited to myself and friends throughout the years, liked girls. Alana and Caroline were slightly confused about the news, too, but they did not judge the circumstances because Anne did not officially announce that she liked girls. Within two weeks, Anne and Jayden called it quits after she explained how abnormal it felt to hold Jayden's hand and calling him a boyfriend. She decided to remain friends with Jayden, and we all continued to hang out.

Around this time, students had to elect recreational activities to participate in such as sports, the arts, or whatever club was offered that year. For the sixth graders, we were able to participate in a few more activities than elementary. Although I knew that I would join chorus for another year by default, I also desired to play a musical instrument. I loved the piano, but school offered lessons for instruments such as the trumpet, clarinet, or even a saxophone. The school provided a small grace period after last period in which students could sort through the instruments, speak to the band teacher, and choose the one that sparked their interest if desired. After school, Anne, Alana, and I went to the band room to sort through the wind instruments, the brass, strings, and percussion. Caroline stood there, disinterested, while we decided on our instrument. The trumpet was difficult for me to get the hang of, and the drums did not give me the same satisfaction as the other instruments. The ultimate verdict was the clarinet, Anne chose the drums, and Alana chose the trumpet. I was extremely excited to be learning something new, especially a new instrument.

As the weeks in school passed, Anne and I continued to remain outside as much as possible before the weather dropped. Since hanging out with Jayden again, we learned that he lived on the way home from school. He introduced us to his friend Kevin who lived a few houses from him and introduced us to his parents as they awaited his arrival from school one day. The first time we met Jayden's parents, they immediately insisted on driving us home because they did not think that it was ideal for two young girls to be walking so far across town from school. I could tell by their body language and concern when they saw us parentless with their son, walking him home without supervision. Alana was with us that day, but she told Jayden's mom that she could meet with her brothers down the road to walk with them. His mom was contented with Alana's response but told her that she would drive her down the street to her brothers' location. She did, and then she dropped us off at home.

Afterward, Jayden told us that his mother would continually insist on driving us unless Alana's brothers remained with us. Instead of walking him directly to his house on Duer, we would stop before his block to say goodbye or walk from a different location. As the days went by, my friendship grew closer to Jayden since we both enjoyed talking a lot, goofing around, and trying to make others laugh. Everyone, meaning Sammie, Caroline, Alana, Anne, and

Kevin, allowed Jayden and me to walk ahead and have some alone time during the walk to and from school. They knew that we liked each other, and something was sparking between us. Although Anne dated Jayden for two weeks, there was no spark and she said that it was weird. Either way, Jayden and I were smitten to see one another every chance we got.

Prior to the story between Jayden and I unfolding, I want to quickly circle back to what happened on my tenth birthday. As mentioned above, my father Chris brought forward the information that I have other siblings, and one of them is a day younger than me. On my birthday, I went to school like normal and my friends arrived with balloons and a gift bag full of candy. Alana and Caroline know that I love candy and chips, as well as anything cheese-flavored such as Cheese-Itz®, cheddar popcorn, or Ritz crackers. All our friends and teachers wished Anne and me a happy birthday and wonderful year ahead. When Anne and I arrived home that evening, Mother was waiting for us. She was happy to see us and took Anne and me to the local diner to celebrate our birthday there. We ate well and had our own slice of cake with a candle on it. Once we got home, Chad went downstairs to hang out with his friends and play poker in the living room. Even though it was the middle of the week, it was normal for Chad and/or Mother to be in their room or downstairs in the living room with plenty of friends, drinks, and music.

As Chad was downstairs, Mother asked us to stay in the bedroom so that she could call our father. I smiled in excitement because the time was finally here for us to meet a new family member, a brother who was the same age as us.

As the phone rang in anticipation for him to pick up, Chris said happy birthday to us and told us to hold on for a second while he grabbed our brother. Once he got on the phone, Father said, "Okay Carla and Anne, this is your brother Chris. Chris's birthday is tomorrow, and he will be ten just like you two. Chris, say hello to them."

I heard the phone shuffle and a minor pause in between, and then my newfound brother said, "Hi, I'm Chris. Nice to meet you. This is so cool that I have twin sisters, hopefully we can meet one day." Mother's phone was loud, but Anne and I had our faces pressed together so that we both could hear every word from the phone.

I responded to Chris and said, "Yeah, me too. Happy almost-birthday to you. I hope you have a great birthday tomorrow!"

Chris answered, "Thank you, and happy birthday to you both. I hope you have a good night." The phone shuffled as I heard him hand the phone back to Father, then he followed up by asking me how excited I was to speak to a newly discovered sibling. Anne and I expressed our own sense of contentment with our little brother Chris and other siblings in Father's house, and we said goodnight to him. Our night was made.

In terms of school life, it was not long until one Monday morning, Jayden saw me in the hallway in between classes and put his arm around me. With onlookers equally curious as to what his next move was, he passed me a paper football-shaped note and asked me to read it when I had a chance. I got to class so I could read the note before the bell rang, and I opened the note as soon as I sat down at my desk. The letter was short, and it went a little something like this:

Hi Beautiful, I hope you are having a good day. I know you like school, so you're probably happy even though I'm not. Anyhow. I have something I want to tell you after school today. Let's talk on the way home. See you soon. Bye, Jayden

On the way home, we initially walked alongside our group of friends to chat before we slowed down to lag for conversation. I was nervous, but ecstatic. Anne stared at me when we paused to slow down, because she had an idea of what Jayden was going to do. As I looked at her, I saw the image in my inner window of Anne talking to Jayden about dating me and if it was okay for us to date. I responded to her face with a blank facial expression, then smiled. Anne nodded, and walked forward with the rest for the crew.

Jayden and I walked silently for a moment as we stared forward. We engaged in casual conversation as he asked me how my day was and if I was happy that we were in a larger school. The conversation seemed to drag on as we walked, which led me to the assumption that Jayden wanted us to speak in a more secluded location about whatever he desired to say. Once we arrived at the corner of the block from the alternate route to his house, he signaled for the others to keep walking so that we could speak secretly. It was cute because I had an idea of where was he going based on his body language, but there was a sense of uneasiness sitting at the pit of my stomach.

Jayden watched as the others walked away and turned back to me with a sincere yet gentle smile. He looked to the pavement on the sidewalk, then looked at me to ask the question. He asked me to be his girlfriend. Although he and Anne and had declared each other boyfriend and girlfriend, it was an eccentric decision that did not go past casual conversation. Jayden looked at Anne some feet ahead, and she looked at me to nod in confirmation that what he was saying was true.

I stared at him, while my twin hollered from down the street, "Bro, just say yes already."

Anne was insinuating something to me by her facial expression and energy. I understood based on her body language that she was truly not into the short-lived relationship. She regarded that relationship as nothing more than friends, thankfully for me. It was October 21st when Jayden asked me to be his girlfriend on the corner of his street.

To quickly reflect on how Jayden asked me to be his girlfriend, I dated Rob, as mentioned previously, and I dated a kid named Julio. Rob and Julio were not emotionally connected to me in the moments we were together, which expectedly was not frequent since we only got to see one another early in the morning or after school and did not seem to be invested in a basic friendship. I found myself trying to pull conversation out of them, trying to engage them in conversation or jokes that I horribly told. I did not want to see another boyfriend of mine act like this. Affectionate attention and human interaction through companionship was something that I craved from my significant other. Julio and Rob did not show me what I craved in a man, but Jayden refocused any wandering thought that I had right back to planet Earth. He completely listened to my ideas and observations on life yet made me laugh. Because even though my life was not normal, I was still present and okay. Maybe I was not getting the best care at home, and I was fearful of when my brother Chris would return home from the military, but he reassured me that I had a different strength that others could not fathom. At ten years old, Jayden was eye to eye with me when I spoke about anything and everything. Although Alana expressed that his personality seemed too goofy for me and that I could do better, we knew there was something different. He was my best friend, but not everyone thought that our relationship would stand a chance.

Towards the middle of fall, Mother told us that she was going to leave the house for a little while, but that she would be back in time. She did not tell us how long she'd be gone or where she was going, but she stated that she may be gone for a week or so on a trip for work. I did not question Mother's whereabouts because a part of me did not care, and a part of me did not know how she could go on a trip for her profession. Anne and I went along with her story and said goodbye to her one morning without hesitation. When we slammed the door behind her, we were so excited that we would be in the house with Chad, Giovanna, and sometimes Eric whenever he made it by the house. As mentioned earlier, Chad tended to drink heavily into the night from the moment he got home. His concern did not revolve around us once we revealed to him our whereabouts and plans. I did not lie to Chad because he was not my father and he did not judge Anne and me for being out in the streets. He trusted that we knew to get around the streets in our city, as well as could protect ourselves and knew where to go if something were to happen. On the other hand, maybe he was not concerned about our whereabouts because he was too under the influence to care.

After Mother was gone, a few days passed and food in the kitchen from the pantry to the cabinets to the refrigerator was running scarce. My creativity was at an all-time high with making a meal and using any ingredient that I had in the kitchen. At the time, regarding food, I had the philosophy that if the food item did not smell or look moldy, it was edible. Over a week or two of time, the food throughout the house, including the staples, ran out. There was no more food in the cabinets, and it was then that I remembered that Mother's purse was not here. Anne and I could not access her debit card or money, and we did not have a cell phone to call Eric. Giovanna was not around recently because she was usually working at the pet store until close on most nights. Including school nights, Giovanna walked across town after work and arrived home as late as midnight sometimes. Giovanna usually coordinated with one of Alana's brothers or a friend to walk home with her. She did not know the extent of the issue at home because she was not around enough to notice the lack of food. Keep in mind that Chris was in the military, so that left Anne and I nothing to eat.

None of us had a pre-purchased school lunch plan because Mother did not believe in paying a school for lunch every day, which typically left us to prepare something ourselves in the morning and eat whatever was available in the house. With that said, with Mother gone, Anne and I went through our first evening and the following morning without food. For the following two days, Chad was in and out of the house so much and drank himself to sleep shortly after arriving home, that we were unable to ask him for money or food. We scavenged through Chris's room that evening and other parts of the house in search for coins. We found three quarters to split between us. We were unsure of the next time we would see Eric or Giovanna again, or how long this would last before telling someone.

The following morning, Anne and I used two quarters to buy one small juice and one small bag of chips on the way to school. This purchase left us with one quarter, but there were two of us. Alana noticed that morning in the convenience store on Somerset Street that we only bought two items for the two of us, and she watched us split it along the way. Alana did not say anything to us or offer to split her food with us, because she received two quarters a morning herself. Essentially, this was our breakfast every morning since walking in this direction to the high school.

Jayden and his friends very rarely walked us to school because Jayden's mother drove them most of the time. That morning Jayden and friends did not meet us on Greenbrook Road to walk to school, so it was just the three of us. Once we approached the high school campus, Anne wandered off in the opposite direction we were walking to see a friend.

Alana and I were walking alongside the school campus towards the entrance for our class when she asked me, "What's been going on with you? I'm noticing that you have been quiet lately and that's not like you. I know you, Carla. I know something is up and you're not telling me. Are you okay?"

I looked down to the pavement as we walked on the sidewalk and sighed as an initial response to her concerns.

She continued, "You guys split a juice and a bag of chips this morning instead of having your own. Is your mom having issues with money or something like that?"

I stared at the ground in frustration and embarrassment of the endless mishaps occurring in my house. She knew that Mother was sweet to her, but she knew the stories of how she neglected us as a parent and slipped into a depression after Kenneth and Elma passed. Alana knew that something was up but couldn't put her finger on it.

As I continued to gaze into the pavement, I finally said to Alana, "My mother has been gone for two weeks and her work sent her away. She's been gone, but we ran out of food. Chad is never there, and when he is, he's sleeping or doesn't answer the door. Anne and I split the chips and juice this morning because we haven't eaten anything else in three days."

Alana then exclaimed, "You haven't eaten in three days? Why didn't you tell me that you are starving? Why didn't your mom leave money behind for him to buy food?!" As she spoke loudly, I looked at our surroundings to see two teachers getting out of their cars, and others walking behind us.

My eyes widened as Alana asked me questions, as it was obvious that she was completely appalled by my issue at hand. One teacher met my eyes from the parking lot in concern for what he just heard Alana say. I was mortified when I observed the reaction of the teachers in the nearby parking lot. It reminded me of how the CPS came due to the whole ordeal of Chris's molestation, and how poorly Mother reacted. I did not want to see the CPS at my house again or Mother upset that I told someone I was starving. In my head, I already envisioned the wrath stemming from Mother and the temperature in my chest began to rise. There was so much guilt building up my chest and throat as I responded to Alana.

Once I gathered my thoughts, I slowly but quietly said, "Except for the chips and juice I just had with Anne, we have not eaten a meal in three days. We only have had water at home from the kitchen sink, and I don't know. I didn't want to worry you. I knew that you would be mad, and I did not want to burden you with something like that. I don't know what she left behind for him, to be honest."

Surprised, Alana widened her eyes and pressed her lips together in response to what I said. She sighed, and said, "Look, Carla. I think you telling me that you're starving is a little more serious than anything else. You need food to live, Carla. More than anything, you should be able to tell me ANYTHING, and I mean that!" I looked diagonally behind me where the teachers parking lot was and noticed the two teachers watching us and listening to the conversation.

I looked back, and I nodded to Alana on what she said. My mind was racing, and I could not initially respond. Moments before we arrived to where all of our friends were waiting to go into the building for school, I stared forward and said, "I'll talk to you more, I guess. I don't know … I'm just scared. Thanks, Alana, I love our friendship."

I did not eat lunch that day either because Anne and I did not have anything to pack and bring. I kept myself busy during lunch and forgot that I hadn't eaten by chatting to everyone and drinking from the water fountain.

That evening, I arrived home and was completely famished. I walked into the house, went to my room, and stared at the ceiling, trying not to think about how hungry I was. I thought about what was left in the kitchen, and I thought that I should maybe have some sugar water if there was sugar, or something to make sure that I had some nutrients in my body. I sighed at the thought of how I should conserve my energy unless I absolutely needed to move around. Was I sure there was something I could scavenge downstairs in a cupboard or the fridge? I knew that Anne was downstairs in the living room, and I made my way down to talk to her about the next steps on our quest to eat. Slowly, I arose from the bed and walked downstairs to the kitchen.

Anne followed me to the kitchen to see what I was up to, and she said, "What are you doing, you going to see what we can whip together in this place? Looks like nothing is here." I turned on the kitchen light and saw about fifty roaches scatter to hide away in any corner they could, and I immediately got itchy under my skin. I did not forget about the roaches, but it was moments like that I was reminded that nothing was safe here. Through time, I learned that roaches get into everything, and it's absolutely disgusting.

Moments later, I heard a knock at the front door, and someone walked in. It was Eric, and I could not be any happier to see his face. I knew that Eric would be able to help us with our food situation, but I could not reach out to him beforehand and tell him. I did not want to make him panic similarly to how Alana did that morning, so

I initially played cool. He smiled and asked how things are going, but he also said that we look like something is wrong.

Anne blurted out, "We are hungry, so freaking hungry. Thank God you are here!"

He looked at me in distress, and said, "Is this true, that you both have not eaten today?" I slowly nodded in relief.

Eric was here, in the flesh, and ready to do anything he could to ensure that we were safe in his presence. He immediately told us to get in his car for us to go grab food immediately, and then we headed to McDonald's. On the way there, we explained that we haven't eaten in three days. Eric began to drive even faster to get to the restaurant drive-thru. He told us to order whatever we wanted, since the price of food was not important. Rather, he was mostly concerned about our wellbeing and safety as young children in our familial situation. During the trip to McDonald's, Eric did not say a word about the whereabouts of Mother or Chad, because he prioritized us eating immediately. He knew that we were concerned, too.

When we returned home, Giovanna walked in from work shortly after and asked us what was going on because we had McDonald's. Eric told her that we hadn't eaten in several days, and Giovanna looked at him, confused, as she walked towards the kitchen. Giovanna started to open the cabinets, only to notice that there truly was not much in the house. Based on her reaction to the lack of food, including staples such as milk or bread, I assumed that Giovanna was surviving from the money she received from her job at the pet store to buy food. Giovanna stared at the floor with her eyes widened, in concern about how long this might be an issue. She said to Eric, "Where the fuck is Chad? He needs to know this shit. I love him and all, but why has he not bought food for the house?"

Before Eric responded to Giovanna, there it was. My inner window appeared, ready to deliver an image or flash of what's to come. It showed me the flash images of Mother arriving home abruptly due to the CPS investigating the amount of food we had in our home. The thought of how the information was received came to mind.

I then envisioned the image of me talking to a guidance counselor in the school offices, as the flash ended with me observing the same woman from CPS walking into the room. She was coming in to speak with me, because the teachers heard me. At this point, my inner window closed.

I knew that the teachers from the parking lot already told the guidance counselor at school, and it was only a matter of time until they spoke to me about it. Eric immediately told Giovanna that he did not want to be in the middle of it, that he would return tomorrow to speak to Chad. But he made it clear to us that he did not want to be involved otherwise. Eric walked out of the house and drove home.

The next morning, Eric showed up in the morning with an egg bagel with cream cheese for us to split. He then drove us to school and even grabbed Alana on the way out. He said to us, "Listen, Anne and Carla, I do not know where your Mother is or what Chad is doing, but no matter what happens, you'll always have me as your big brother. I don't come around for anyone else but you two, because you both need someone to be around."

When we arrived at school, Alana thanked Eric for driving us as we exited the car. Halfway through the morning, my teacher received a phone call from the principal's office, and I knew through claircognizance that it was for me. As expected, the teacher instructed me to go to the principal's office. On the walk to the office, my walking pace dramatically slowed down, but on the other hand, the thoughts about the revealing of events from my inner window triggered me into fear of the other unknowns. The built-up guilt of my family's issues filled into an energy balloon full of cement that pressed against my chest. There was no turning back, because I betrayed my family's matters by communicating that I was starving for almost three consecutive days. All of this, due to Mother's unknown absence per work's request, a trip that I did not understand. She never called us, never wrote a letter, or reached out to Chad on her absence. The walk to the office was my strategizing time around how to go about this. I could not make Mother look bad or come off as a child in need of attention.

The secretary of the school was eating a sandwich when I entered the principal's office, and she pointed her finger filled with sandwich residuals to her right where the guidance counselor's office was located. I grinned at her in greeting but quickly looked away in disgust because of her open mouth when she chewed.

I entered the room to see the guidance counselor standing in attendance with the security guard that works in the school. After I entered, the security guard walked out.

The guidance counselor, Mr. Thyme, said hello and asked me to have a seat in his office. I nodded and sat.

He said, "I have seen you and your twin in the hallways, and you are both quite outgoing to the students, no matter the age. It is a pleasure to have you in this office today. How are you feeling today, is everything alright?"

I stared at him in acknowledgement that I knew where this was going and played along. I said, "Yes, Mr. Thyme, everything is okay. I am here, so that's a start, how are you?"

He cut right to the chase due to the time pressing before the others arrived, and said, "I am good, thank you for asking. A day or so ago, one of the high school teachers overheard a conversation that you and a friend were having near the teacher's parking lot. They heard your friend repeat what they believed you may have said to her, which was that you have not eaten in three days. They continued to listen to your conversation due to their concern for your health and safety. They brought this to the staff's attention, which is why you are here. Someone will be in here shortly to speak to you in more detail and understand how we can assess and help the situation."

Shortly after, the security guard knocked on the door and the CPS worker gently entered the room. It was the same woman that I saw in my inner window yesterday evening. The energy in the room became grounded, like an authoritative body representing its client in court; it was protective yet one-sided. As I projected, she began to ask questions about my statements to Alana to read my body language, energy, and validity of information. The CPS worker was completely analyzing me, and I knew that the conversation had in this office would eventually lead to a check with Mother and Chad. She asked me where my mother went, and I told her that she went away under work's orders. It was not a business trip, but rather, something that I could not put my finger on, until I saw her facial expression based on my answer.

She looked at the guidance counselor as if I was completely invisible and said, "It sounds like her mom is in rehab or something if work sent her, but it's not a business trip? Sort of like a vacation? Something does not sound right." She looked at me and thanked me for the information. My stomach knotted from her statement, because she was on to something. I realized it may be true, too.

Within ten minutes of being in the guidance counselor's office, Anne was escorted in and asked about Mother's whereabouts and the availability of food in the home. Anne was vague in her responses and seemed frustrated because she knew that the information received from the school and CPS likely came from me. By nature, I have been known to be a Chatty Cathy, and it was likely that Anne already figured out that it was me who said something. The more questions that the CPS representative asked, the less information that Anne provided.

It was only a matter of time before Giovanna was called into the office. When Giovanna arrived ten or so minutes later, she was infuriated to see us in the office with the assumption that we got into trouble. On the other hand, the principal instructed Giovanna to sit down and got her caught up to speed. Once Giovanna understood the reason why Anne and I were there and what they needed to interview her about, she was infuriated. Giovanna stared at me with fire in her eyes as she answered their questions. Giovanna did not have much to say, since she has been out of the house most of the time due to school and working at the pet store until close.

When the questions ended, the guidance counselor exited to quickly get the attention of the security guard in the hallway. He escorted us back to class, walking in silence with him. They dropped me off to class first, and when I entered the room everyone stared at me. I knew that it was only a few hours until school ended, and we would see the CPS worker at the house again.

I stared at the blank worksheet on my desk that was placed there while I was out of the classroom. The thought of what consequences would follow thanks to Alana's loudmouth raced through my head. Every person in my household came to mind, including wondering whether Mother would now come home. What if my older brother Chris came home instead?

I quieted my mind to see if I could gain more information on what may unfold in the afternoon and next few days. Still staring at the blank worksheet on the desk, my inner window finally opened. Totally unfocused to the classroom, the inner window made my forehead feel as though there were hands holding a doorway open to my brain. My focus was as clear as it ever was up to that moment. Here, I saw Mother arriving home abruptly after CPS showed up, her mental state in shambles, crying in her bedroom. There was conflict within Mother and her mental state deteriorating within weeks of her return. No words were spoken in the vision, but instead I heard a disheartening background noise of screeches and screams ringing through my head. The noises set the tone of her mental state for the vision, as if she was going mad after her return. I closed my eyes to eliminate the vision and sounds. I opened my eyes moments later to refocus on the blank worksheet in hopes of finishing it before the bell rang. As I completed the last multiple-choice question, the bell rang. I apologized to the teacher for being the last one to hand it in, and I walked out before she questioned me.

Anne and I walked home with Alana and everyone per usual, but Anne was clearly angry and sarcastically replying to Alana throughout the walk home. Jayden asked me if everything was okay, since he saw me, Anne, and Giovanna go to the principal's office during class. I reassured him that the situation was not important, but he didn't believe me. He offered his parents to help figure things out, and I smiled as I shook my head. I told him that I would never involve him in my family's mess. I went home. Giovanna arrived home before us and was cleaning the house. I noticed she was transferring freezer-burned meat, pasta sauce, and vegetables from the freezer into the refrigerator to make it look full. She started opening boxes in the pantry to spread the food out. I did not help her because her strong negative energy seeped through the first floor of the house as she shuffled through the food. I knew that whatever was going to happen when CPS arrived was already in the cards to be played.

I walked upstairs and anticipated their arrival as I opened a textbook from my backpack to start homework. Anne arrived in our room from helping Giovanna downstairs, then I heard three hard knocks at the door. We could see from the top of the stairs that it was the lady from CPS who we saw earlier. Chad made his way down the stairs as he silently motioned for us to keep quiet. I continued to read my textbook because I had to do my homework anyway, and there was nothing I could do in the moment. Moments later, the CPS worker left, and Chad came back upstairs with Eric. Luckily for Chad, Eric happened to show up, and he talked to the CPS worker as a distraction until the worker left. Eric took us to grab dinner at McDonald's again, and he dropped us back off at the house.

Throughout the evening, I stayed awake to read ahead in my textbooks and understand what was coming next in school. The pace at school picked up slightly and I did not want to be behind on the curriculum. Sometime that evening, Mother walked through the front door and I heard her quietly making her way up the stairs. She and Chad went to their room and talked for a little, but I was exhausted from the day and fell asleep shortly afterward.

A few days went by, and Mother's energy state was completely uneasy and confusing towards everyone in the house. There was a new but different mental state in Mother, based on her body language and the tone in which she spoke. I assumed it was a mix of her depression and her health due to her weight gain through the years. Within days of her arrival, Mother asked Anne and I to go to the pharmacy to pick up her prescription.

We got on our bicycle and we took turns standing on the pegs as we made our way across town. Once we arrived, the gentleman behind the counter knew we were there to pick up her medicine, and without saying a word, handed us a white paper bag with three prescription bottles inside. Surprisingly, Mother asked us to return days later to pick up more prescriptions. When she called me into her bedroom, I was able to slip her debit card in my pocket while she was laying in her bed with her back to me and breathing heavy as she asked us to go to the pharmacy again. During the bike ride there, Anne and I rode silently as she thought the same question I had: why were we going to the pharmacy again? Moreover, it was strange we were going to meet with the same person working behind the counter around the same time in the evening, just before closing. At the pharmacy, the man behind the counter handed us a bag, and we ventured to the bank to grab some cash. After school the next day, we grabbed some food at Acme to get us through a week or so.

Throughout the week, I thought about the man behind the counter at the pharmacy and the mysterious connection between him and Mother. Maybe it was because Mother was a chemist, and although she was ill, maybe he gave her a discount because she was a friend of his. Something in me did not accept it at face-value.

By this time, my twin and I were ending our first year in intermediate school and had lived through ten years of life endured in gross form. These ten years consisted of strength, laughter, loss, and encounters that I had not shared with my friends. Jayden had been a soft support and listener to this point, but I knew he could not understand the darkness and depth of the rooted issues that caused such turmoil within the energy of my home. Based on what I knew of Jayden, he could not fathom the spirits or people and their dynamics in my family and household. The only part of me that I revealed to my friends and Jayden was that I could communicate with and envision spirits within and without my inner window. They knew that I could see images and warning signs in future states without teaching myself how to. I could not control this gift. This to me, is the definition of *Triggers are the Guides*. My guides so far, Kenneth, Elma, and Jesus, have shed light upon my sight to help see the trigger before it's released.

In addition to Mother's worsening mental state and ambiguities in her tendencies, such as her previous whereabouts, the dark spiritual occurrences and energies continued to push through the space of our household. The spiritual energy in the house remained intense, as it did not beg to differ the circumstances of Mother's state of being. We'd lived for approximately six years in the house at Forestbrook Drive. Since our arrival, Mother had not done much to spiritually clean the house. At the time, I did not know what it meant to spiritually clean the house, but I knew that we needed the cleaning. I thought about how people could not have possibly resided in haunted homes like ours that had such dense energy, and nothing could be done to clean up the place. I saw the *Exorcist* movie one evening on the weekend with my siblings, and I would think a house clearing is something like that. In the movie, I recall a priest going to the house to eradicate the evil spirits in the house. When thinking of Mother, maybe she did not know how to deal with dark energies and spirits, but it was also possible that the energies never impacted her in the house—until now.

One evening, I was sound asleep in my bed, for once in a long time. That day, I did not encounter any disruptions from my siblings, the spiritual energy floating through the house, or from Chad listening to the TV extremely loud. Around three o'clock in the morning, my twin and I were abruptly awoken by screams coming from Mother's bedroom. We heard her run out of her bedroom, and quickly learned when we opened our bedroom doors that she was naked in terror. She was holding onto a throw blanket to try and cover herself as she ran out, but I was more concerned as to why she ran out of her bedroom like a bat out of hell.

She quickly turned and bolted down the stairs. Chad followed her down the stairs in equal terror, and by the look on his face, he also experienced the same thing. When Mother made it down the stairs, we followed her in panic that someone could be in her bedroom. No one was there. Instead, she told us that she saw a spirit that looked like a little boy in her bedroom, and it morphed into the body of the air conditioner. After the little boy disappeared momentarily, a priest wearing "his full uniform with the precious white miter on his head and jet-black eyes" morphed out of the air conditioner. As she explained in a terrified manner, the priest was speaking in tongues to her and raising his voice as he morphed form the air conditioner. The dark-spirited priest looked nothing like the boy who morphed into the air conditioner, according to Mother. When she finally calmed down downstairs, it was four o'clock in the morning. She asked Anne to sleep on the neighboring couch with her in the living room, while Chad and the rest of us returned upstairs to sleep for a few hours.

The next morning, Mother stayed home from work and went to the nearby church to consult with the priest about the issues we had been having in the house. I recall coming home from school that day and Mother and Giovanna were spraying olive oil on the walls of Giovanna's room, repeatedly whispering, "I rebuke you in the name of Jesus Christ." I watched them from the hallway as one proceeded to my bedroom, and the other made her way into the hallway.

When I saw them enter Chris's room, Mother opened a bottle of holy water from the church. She began to shake the bottle of holy water on the walls and chant the phrase. I immediately sensed my body feeling pressure and heat external to my skin. Something was there. It was in my vicinity, and it felt as though someone wrapped me in multiple sleeping bags and placed me in an oven. It was as if my breath didn't exist, and the air was filling in my lungs. I exhaled as I watched them cleanse the space, and I noticed that I pushed harder than usual to feel the air exit my lungs. On the surface, I was calm as I stared at Giovanna and Mother. They must have felt the spiritual intensity, too, as they began to shout the chants from the top of their lungs. A simple house cleansing was beginning to feel like an energy battle between Mother and Giovanna, and the spiritual presence we could not identify.

The front door burst open from below and I looked downstairs to see someone I was not expecting. The priest from our church arrived, and he was already running up towards the commotion. He lifted his arms with his palms facing the ceiling as he started to pray loudly into the room. The priest projected his voice into Chris's room in attempts to calm the space. There was no change in the denseness of the section of the house we were in. I stared at him in panic because of the lack of control the priest showed in the situation. Moments later, I heard a scream.

I looked around the room to see the screaming was coming directly from Giovanna, who was inside of Chris's room. She was in the eye of the spiritual storm. Giovanna's screaming regressed into a sound that I have never heard before, with growls and mumbling in tandem. The mumbling of words was in a different language. The priest immediately focused his energy on Giovanna, because based on the way her behavior quickly changed, she may have been possessed.

I stood in the hallway in bewilderment of what was unfolding before my eyes. None of my guides had arrived to help with the situation like the last time. So, I intuitively walked down to the living room where Anne was sitting peacefully as things unfolded upstairs. I wanted to allow things upstairs to potentially dissipate.

Upstairs, within minutes, Giovanna was able to quiet down. Expectedly, Giovanna was not mentally stable in any way. The priest hurriedly left after Giovanna settled down, purposefully before the energy intensified in the house again. Before he left, I heard him reassure Mother that he would return to continue attenuating the spirits and energy.

That evening, I laid in bed in reflection of what occurred that day, constantly wondering about why my spirit guides did not come to help during the time that the priest was present. Isn't this why loved ones and Jesus showed up for me in the past, to help me when I was in need and provide advice and guidance for circumstances before they worsen? It did not make sense. My twin and I shared the bed that evening in case the residual energy of dark spirits decided to bother us. We did not speak about what transpired that evening, especially since Anne stayed out of it and remained downstairs. I was awakened by my own thoughts in the middle of the night. I thought about my life thus far, and the mental instability of everyone in the household. There was a calm sense of stillness in my body as I laid on my back and stared at the ceiling, reflecting on what life in my first decade consisted of. I remembered how my spirit felt utterly focused on my journey forward, no matter what was to come next. I needed to remain strong.

Mother attempted to call the church in search of the priest a few times after that day, but he never returned her phone calls. After the ordeal, the energy in the house deepened into a state of desolation, and we felt every ounce of it. Every morning I woke up to a conflicted feeling that each new day was an opportunity to have a beautiful day, yet there was this sense of despair and pain that lingered in the household energy. The energy seeped into my pores as I got ready for school in the house, and I had to make an effort to hurry out of that home every morning. Whenever I arrived home from school and was hanging out with Jayden or my friends, upon entering the front door, I was showered with sadness in the air.

Around this time, my twin and I frequently eavesdropped at the crack of the bedroom door, because we needed to understand more about Mother. We both knew that there was sorrow in Mother's heart due to her losses, but we knew that there was more she was hiding. Mother carried an eerie tension and depression that she had. Whenever we snooped at her door, we had a particular method in how we eavesdropped. One of us remained away from her door to be aware of the surroundings, such as the front door or someone coming up the stairs to avoid getting caught. It was best for us to listen in whenever Giovanna was at work and Eric didn't come by to hang out with Chad, especially in the early evening around dinnertime. It was not long until we started putting together the pieces, slowly but surely, to understand what Mother was going through.

From the crack of her doorway, Anne and I took turns listening to their conversations pertaining to issues around paying the mortgage due to the immense amount of bills Mother had to pay. There was a comment made about moving out of the house before the bank came and took everything. We did not know that they meant taking assets that belonged to Mother, but we understood it as all her furniture, items of ours, and possibly the expensive clothes that Mother bought for her and Chad. She explained to Chad that she needed to get out of this debt and needed to let the house go into foreclosure. We heard her confirm that she would be filing bankruptcy that week, and they'd need to look for a place for everyone to live. Mother's tone exemplified anger as she spoke to Chad, and it was obvious that everything in life (spiritual, mental, emotional, physical) was impacting her to full force.

Within weeks of the incident, Anne and I came home from hanging out with friends, and Alana accompanied us. Mother heard us come in and came downstairs to greet us in her pajamas. We were happy to see her come out to greet Alana, but Anne and I noticed her demeanor was quite serious. She hugged Alana and said hello, but then looked at us to say, "You need to go upstairs and start packing. We will need to be out of this house in a week. Alana, we have a lot to do to get this house cleared out. We won't be going far, and you can still see the twins. Feel free to stay around and help pack if you'd like."

I stared at Mother in shock and said, "What? Wait, why are we leaving?" She completely ignored my response and looked at Alana, looked down, then proceeded upstairs to her bedroom. We told Alana that we could hang out another time, and she nodded in agreement. Alana hugged us and left in shock, because she knew that we would be leaving before the seventh grade started. Even worse, we'd leave before the summer was over, so I wouldn't have time to say bye to friends at school.

Mother explained to us that we needed to pack all our clothes because we had to bomb the house due to the roach problem. I mentioned before that when the Garrettsons moved into our house, we had an infestation of roaches ever since. Mother told us that we would be back in the house in a week or so, and that we would all need to stay in a temporary house until then.

I was frustrated because of the unexpected news, and I knew that I had to tell my friends I was moving. Although the roaches were Mother's reason for us leaving, I knew in my heart that we were leaving for other reasons. I had a knot in my stomach as we packed because I knew that we were never coming back to this house. In a sense there was a relief because of the spiritual energy that lingered before our arrival, but I was nervous about the change of moving to a new space. It was fear of the unknown. I knew the issue with the roach infestation was minuscule compared to the complexity of what was flustering Mother's spirit and overall state of being. There was so much happening in Mother's life and therefore ours as well, but it was evident that her personal experience with the morphing spirit in her bedroom was the final incident that pushed her decision to move out. The priest coming to assist was a failed attempt in attenuating the spiritual forces in the home. We knew that we were additionally moving because of the mortgage payments; the overall dark energy in the house experienced by us and outside friends, and other debts from Kenneth, were other reasons for our departure. Within weeks of the priest's attempt at house-clearing, we were out of one house and into a new house located on a corner two towns over.

We moved to a town called Dunellen, to a desolate corner of a busy road near the town border on South Ave. When we arrived at the Dunellen house, I memorized the way to get there to ensure that I could ride my bicycle back to my hometown to visit friends. Because it was the early twenty-first century, we did not have cell phones to call our friends and chat.

As we were transporting our belongings from the Forestbrook house to the South Ave. house, I thought about Jayden, because he was away in Florida visiting his grandmother for the month of August. I was unable to say goodbye to him upon my departure, and I wanted him to know. Jayden obviously didn't know I was leaving and would not find out until he came home. One of my friends would have to tell him. My heart sank at the thought of him, because I wanted him to know now and I didn't want him to find out through a friend instead. I did not want Jayden to think that I came from a disorganized and confusing family, full of ad hoc decisions based on one mother of four's judgement. Truly, it was my fear that Jayden would perceive instability in my household when he found out that I abruptly moved like this. Jayden's parents always had their eye on Mother's lack of supervision, noting my freedom to do whatever I wanted, like being out in the streets at all times of the day and night.

It was a few weeks before school started when we moved in. My twin and I took a few trips to North Plainfield and made the necessary rounds so our friends would know we relocated temporarily but also that we were still around. Anne and I had no idea what "temporary" meant, but this is what Mother continuously said as we packed our items to leave the Forestbrook Drive house. When my twin and I rode our bikes to our hometown the first time, the bicycle ride took us about thirty minutes. We decided to ride to Caroline's house as a first stop since we knew she'd be home. Caroline informed us that Alana already told her and Sammie the other day, so we decided to see if we could find anyone else around town to let them know of our departure. We rode to the Greenbrook Park on the way back to Dunellen, since it was on the west side of town. We didn't see any friends there, so we went back towards the South Ave. house.

As Anne and I biked our way into the town of Dunellen, we noticed that the main street had an arcade that looked interesting from the outside. We stopped our bikes to peek into the window of the place, to see there were pool tables and arcade games like Pac-Man and Nascar. We wanted to see what else this arcade may have in store, so Anne and I rode to the back of the building to leave our bikes. Since we didn't have locks for our bicycles, we left them in the back without locking them. We made our way inside and saw that there was an area to order finger foods like cheesesteaks and fries, and an immense machine nearby that someone was playing on. This immense machine was like no other that we have seen. The player on the gaming machine, a male, was stepping on arrows located on the floor to align with the music playing on the screen. I knew that the game was directly related to the music because of the way he stepped on the arrows to the beat of the song playing, and I was completely intrigued. Anne walked over to the machine to stand by him as he played. She turned to look at me while it was still playing, and she said, "Carla, this machine has two players. We can both play!"

When the song finished, Anne asked the guy on the machine if she could play the next round. The game required three quarters per player, but neither of us had a single quarter to play. The guy looked at us and knew that we likely did not have money to play. He looked at Anne, and he said, "What's your name? My name is Sheldon. I got one of you for a game." My twin looked at me, and I nodded in confirmation for her to utilize the free game from Sheldon to try it out. Sheldon played a slower song for Anne's first time and set her up at easy level, and he set his playing level at expert.

They played three games, and I was unquestionably amazed by the amount of fun she had in such a short amount of time. I was amped watching her play each game and saw how quickly she understood as played the game. Since Anne and I played the drums and clarinet, respectively, in the school band, we were used to following the pace and becoming familiar with the rhythm of songs, so playing an arcade game to reflect music was a sweet spot. As mentioned before, we also had a passion for video games in playing the Game Boy and N64. As Anne played with Sheldon on the platform, I was smiling in thought of the fresh endeavor we were about to pursue. How divine was it that a video game, here in this arcade, was designed to make you move to the beat of a song using your feet, and so close to the South Ave. house? This was a perfect hobby to keep us busy during our temporary time away from North Plainfield.

After the second song, Sheldon informed Anne that the third song was the last one for them. She turned to me and said, "I think you should play the last song. Try it out. This shit is so much fun." Ecstatic and nervous, I stepped on the game platform. Anne said, "Put your feet on the arrows so you can get familiar with how it feels and the spacing." As I started to move my feet around, I noticed the arrows lit up when I stepped on each arrow for visibility. I liked that the arrows on the platform illuminated while Sheldon sifted through the menu on the game. Before he selected the song, he practiced a few fast motions by stepping on several arrows within seconds, using both of his feet in preparation to play.

We played the third song, and it was so much fun getting the hang of the game. I truly believe this was due to the natural rhythm my twin and I had from loving music and instruments. We both understood how songs are broken down, from pace to the importance of the hook of each piece of music. We thanked Sheldon for letting us play a game with him and went back to our bikes to head home. It was dark outside by our bicycles, but we were happy that the bikes were untouched.

In the darkness, we made our way home a few blocks away. We finally arrived on our street, about half a block away from the house, when we noticed a group of girls across the street sitting on the porch and sharing laughs together. As we rode by, Anne said hello when there was a break of silence in their shared laughter.

The girls smiled and invitingly said hello back.

Anne pointed to our house as she said to the girls, "We just moved here from North Plainfield, we live here."

The girl sitting in the middle said, "Okay, well I live right here, so we can all chill if you want."

Anne responded, "Okay, we'll see you tomorrow then. Nice to meet you!" As I rode behind Anne, watching her initiate a potential friendship, I smiled and waved in harmony to the conversation ending.

The remainder of the summer consisted of playing at the arcade daily using borrowed quarters from Mother's large five-gallon coin jar and traveling on bicycles to our hometown to see our friends. Jayden did not come back from vacation until the week before the school year started. I used the house phone to call his house a few times, but I was not comfortable leaving a voice message for his entire family to hear. I had to depend on Caroline, Kevin, or Alana to let Jayden know of my temporary departure. I was able to inform Kevin, Jayden's best friend, when I saw him one day when he was playing basketball at Greenbrook Park in the summer.

The next day, the girl who lived across the street came outside when she saw Anne and I playing in the backyard. The South Ave. house was on the corner, and since there was no fence, she could easily see the yard from her house. She approached us and waved to announce her presence. She said, "I figured I would come by, because I see you both are outside. I'm Gabriela, by the way."

Anne responded, "I'm Anne, and this is Carla."

I smiled as she approached us and shook her hand in excitement, happy to meet a new friend. She asked us questions to get to know us and keep the conversation going. She told us about herself, in that her family was from Colombia and they loved to party. We giggled because Anne and I equally loved to party, too; to us, that meant especially loud music and dancing with the music.

Our new friend Gabriela hung out with us for the remainder of the summer in between our trips to North Plainfield and the arcade. We met her parents, and she met ours. My mother loved her how she adored Alana and Caroline. Mother allowed us to sleep over at her house on the weekends to party with her family. We were introduced to Spanish music and the different genres within the world of Latin music, which I never knew existed. I immediately fell in love with Latin music and downloaded the songs and burned new CDs for the house. We had recently asked Mother for a small stereo system as a joint birthday gift to enjoy listening to music in our bedroom. Thankfully before our birthday, Mother bought us a bookshelf stereo to enjoy listening to music on our own terms.

Anyway, on the first day of school, Gabriela and her friends walked with us and introduced us to her other friends at the middle school, and we quickly became known as the twins from North Plainfield. Although we made several friends through Gabriela's outgoing personality, there was a sense of loneliness each day as I entered school. The feeling of being away from my friends in my hometown and Jayden felt like a bad dream that I couldn't wake up from.

Regarding the other aspects of life at the time, such as Mother, a few things changed in Mother's behavior since our move to Dunellen. She recently joined a church nearby with Giovanna and would have us all go to bible study with her in the evenings. On Sundays we went to attend church. I did not mind going because I loved the sense of holiness piercing through me as I listened to prayer, songs, and the love of light in the church. This church was unlike the Catholic church in North Plainfield, and it was because I learned that this church was of Christian beliefs. This was the first time that I learned the churches could be different in worship. From my observations, the two main differences were that the Christian church did not do mid-mass offerings, and there was more singing of songs like attending a concert. The Catholic church, on the other hand, usually had an organ playing and the people of the church sang like angels in the sky. Either way, it was a wonderful time to celebrate my guide Jesus on Sunday mornings.

I enjoyed going to church because I wanted to understand Jesus, what his life consisted of, and why we were here on this Earth now. Mother and Giovanna got close to the church community and began attending several times a week, and they dragged us with them whenever we did not resist. Since Mother had us there several times a week, I asked her if I could do singing lessons with a lady at the church to strengthen my voice. She agreed because the singing lessons occurred at the same time as when she went to a class there during the week. Anne did not want singing lessons, but she played around with the guitar and drums in the main room where worship occurred, while Mother attended the weekly class. We weren't sure why Mother attended weekly evening sessions, but we went to hang in the church. It was the first time Mother let me do something extracurricular that was not school related, something that possibly cost her money to do.

At home, the spiritual energy in the house decreased significantly since moving to Dunellen. It was tolerable compared to the Forestbrook house, and certainly more peaceful than what we encountered a few months prior. There were a few evenings that I would see a lingering spirit in the evenings, but it wasn't the kind of spirit that brought the energy of the house to a top-notch level of scary. When I would see these spirits, which usually came here and there, I acknowledged its presence by letting it know I could see him/her and would fall asleep with no problem. I mentioned earlier in the book that Chris encountered the most powerful entity in the house that made him paint his room red. According to Chris, the name of the entity that he encountered several times and made him behave strangely started with the letter "L." In Dunellen, it was nice to see a lingering spirit here and there throughout the night instead of experiencing the instilled fear of waking up to a spirit in proximity.

In terms of my communications with my spirit guides, so far to be Kenneth, Elma, and Jesus, I did not see them as much as I did in the other house, but rather, in this timeframe I began to have dreams with them in it. In the dreams, I would receive a message for me as guidance or warning, and sometimes insight for the future. This was a new way of receiving information from them, but I was thankful to see previews of what would happen within a few day's timeframe ahead.

On our eleventh birthday in October, Mother allowed for Anne and me to throw a birthday party in the South Ave. house and invite our friends from our hometown. Mother knew that we missed our friends, and this was her way of letting us connect our hometown friends with our new friends. Since Mother gave us the bookshelf stereo before the party, we set up our bedroom for dancing. We moved all the dressers to the corner and put our bed up on the wall. It was not the first party we ever had for Anne and me, but this one was the first large one, since our friends from both towns were showing up to celebrate with us. Gabriela arrived early to set up, and both Alana and Caroline came soon after in Grandma's car. Mother seemed ecstatic to see Alana and Caroline, as well as some of my friends who she never met, including my boyfriend Jayden who was dropped off by his dad. Mother cooked spaghetti Bolognese for us that evening while we danced to music in the bedroom and outdoor porch area. Thankfully, my hometown friends got along with my new Dunellen friends, until the space we were in got overcrowded and people got rowdy. Jayden was bothered by one of the Dunellen boys trying to dance with me constantly and Kevin got involved.

The next thing I knew, Kevin and Gabriela were outside yelling at the boy. I noticed that Kevin was holding a large tree branch and swinging it like a baseball bat. Jayden was standing a few feet from Kevin in the yard, not trying to fight, but rather antagonizing the situation from a small distance. Someone called the cops due to the commotion outside, and all my friends dispersed. It was a fun night of partying, but I never forgot how Jayden reacted to the situation. Jayden appeared to be protective of me through observing Kevin and Gabriela yelling at the boy on his behalf. I appreciated Jayden's softness, but he was not as aggressive in that moment as I would have hoped for. He let Kevin take over the situation, but I wanted Jayden to get involved.

It was not long until Anne and I returned to our hometown on our bikes in the beginning of fall, within two weeks of our birthday bash. It was a fall morning on a Saturday as we made our way through the town of Greenbrook as an alternative, since that route was not as dangerous as riding bicycles through the ghettos of Plainfield. As we calmly rode through the outskirts of Greenbrook into the edge of North Plainfield, my twin rode her bike ahead of me. As I was riding on the main road, trying to catch up to Anne, a station wagon made a right turn and completely dismissed my presence riding across the street in broad daylight. The car hit the left side of my body and I was thrown a few feet to the pavement.

The street I was riding on was a busy street, and the highway Route 22 ran perpendicular to it. There were cars coming when my body hit the pavement, and thankfully the first car that was in the lane I was in saw me and stopped. She did not allow any cars to pass behind her because I was still laying there. I yelled for Anne because I was scared, realizing that I could not stand up easily because I was in complete shock. My body felt like I had pins and needles shooting through my bloodstream. My right wrist was especially throbbing in pain and appeared red in color due to the impact. I must have put my hands out to break my fall, because I did not hit my head, but rather my right hand and side. Thankfully, I was conscious and not hurt badly.

The man who hit me got out of the car and stared at me, then he apologized.

The woman who stopped the traffic instructed me not to move from where I was standing as she called the police. She told the man to get back in the car and if he leaves, she will report him to the police as a hit-and-run driver.

As I watched the man's reaction to her stern words, I noticed that his behavior was strange, and he seemed a little out of the ordinary. My inner window, which I had not seen in a long time, came forward, and I envisioned the image of him sitting at his kitchen table in solitude. The inner window provided me information on the man acting peculiar before our eyes. This man was just drinking liquor at the kitchen table with his breakfast.

I watched him get back into the car, and my inner window dissipated. There was a tear coming from my eye from the shock and frustration of how my day would continue, with the police coming and Mother possibly getting called. I lowered my eyebrows in thought. I stared at the man in his car, waiting for police to arrive, as I connected with his solitude and felt the sadness in his heart. He knew that he hit me on my bicycle while driving with alcohol in his system, and he felt uneasy and nervous about the consequences.

When the police came, I vividly recall the policeman asking him how much he had to drink, because his breath smelled of alcohol. I turned away to look at the woman, who then asked me if I was okay. She stood with the policeman until he dismissed her. I believe that the woman who supported me likely had a child or little sister, because she was genuinely concerned about my wellbeing.

No cars beeped or caused mayhem that morning due to the traffic building up on the street. As the policeman filed the report, I felt a global sense of security from the cars passing, the police, and the woman's presence.

Anne finally turned around and came to where I was. She sat on the curb and asked if I was okay, but she did not say much else. Anne continued to stare at the man speaking to the policeman, which I think may have prompted him to ask us for a parent's number. I gave him the house phone, and he dialed home. Chad picked up the phone, and he and Mother soon arrived at the scene.

It was critical for Chad to come along, to ensure Mother did not yell at the man who hit me while I was riding, because he knew that she was not pleased to be called over to the scene of an accident. Mother arrived and spoke to me and the policeman, as Chad stood behind her in anticipation of the rage coming through her teeth. Chad put my bicycle in the car as the ambulance brought me to the hospital to fully assess all injuries. I did tell the policeman and the EMT in the ambulance that it was only my wrist that bothered me, but they insisted that I follow the protocol to get checked. When the hospital officially determined my wrist was sprained and nothing else was wrong, they sent me home. Anne rode her bicycle home to meet us later and kept me company since we never made it to our hometown.

In the next few weeks, it started to get colder, and Mother agreed to drive us to our hometown one time while she visited Chad's family in Plainfield, since I couldn't bike over there until my wrist got better. By the time my wrist healed, it was rounding out into winter break.

The Return to our Hometown

During the winter break, Mother instructed us to start packing our bedrooms and helping her with the kitchen since we were moving back to North Plainfield. I was excited that we were moving back to town. However, I wondered if we were really going back to the old house as Mother mentioned when we left. Mother never mentioned the old house until we arrived at the new house on Watchung Ave., which was a few blocks away from the Forestbrook house. The Watchung house was nothing like the other homes we lived in, because now we were on one of the busiest streets in town. Mother officially mentioned to Anne and me that she had to file bankruptcy due to the fictitious checks made out by Kenneth and her debt from medical bills. I did not know enough to understand what the medical bills were, but in reflection I perceived that her health was declining, and it cost a lot of money to stay afloat. When we finally moved to the Watchung Ave. house in the beginning of January, we were able to be with our friends again. Alana lived a little over a block in the opposite direction now, and Caroline was a little farther than before, since she was no longer a block up the street.

Within a week of arriving, since it was still the holiday break, we drove to see Pop in southern New Jersey and visited Chad's family in Plainfield. As Mother drove south, down the Garden State Parkway and into the desolate beach towns towards my Pop's house, she was scarily silent, but I knew her mind was racing. There was something that stressed her as we drove down to his house, but I would not know or understand until we arrived. Chad was quiet in the car and stared forward in thought, too, and it made me wonder if there was potentially an issue that we were walking into when we arrived at Pop's. I looked around the backseat and noticed Anne playing with her Game Boy Color. Giovanna was reading something, and so I proceeded to gaze out of the window. Watching the cars and the trees passing as Mother raced down the parkway, my inner window appeared. It displayed images of Mother arguing with Pop, as the anger raged within her due to Pop's judgement of Mother. Because of this judgement, Mother stormed out in hostility. Pop seemed to have concern for her health and wellbeing, which caused us to leave abruptly without a proper goodbye. These images in the inner window provided the warning I needed to see, in preparation for what would transpire at Pop's house.

The initial arrival to Pop's house was a normal one—my cousins Paul and Rob were in the house with Pop, and the other family members were at Aunt Fran's house next door, gathering and talking. Everyone was so excited to see us arrive for a holiday visit as we brought our bags in the house to stay one night. Chad was quiet, but he introduced himself to Pop as expected. Mother sat down next to Pop. I asked Paul if he would come with us to his house next door to see the others, and on the walk there I asked him how things had been and how school was for him, and per usual, he didn't carry on a conversation. Our other cousin Lauren, who was similar in age, was there to spend time with us. At Aunt Fran's next door, I said hello to everyone at the house, and then I headed back. I wanted to spend time with Pop since I knew what was coming forth, and because I loved listening to his stories about his days in the Navy.

On the short route back to Pop's house next door, we could hear Mother yelling at Pop, saying, "My medication in my bag is what I need to treat my high blood pressure, my depression, and the others are for diabetes. It's a medicine bag."

I heard Pop say to Mother, "Viola, you're telling me that you need a whole bag full of prescription medication to get through the day? You've got to be shitting me, Viola. You can't lie to me; you have a problem, and you need to clean up your act!"

We walked into the house, and he continued, "Look at these beautiful children, look around the room!" He pointed with the cigar in between his fingers at Giovanna to complete his statement. Paul immediately turned around and walked out of the house, without saying a word to anyone about the awkward argument unfolding.

Pop stopped Mother in her tracks as she tried to respond, and he said, "Now, I want you to get out of my house. Take your shit and go. Until I know you are cleaned up again, I am going to give you a hard time until I see the change. So, you make the choice. When it is made, you'll see me again, and I'll see my grandkids again."

She looked at her father and said, "If that's how you want to do it, then I am getting the fuck out of here. You're not going to judge me for something I can't control. I can't even come down here and enjoy a visit with my father. Fuck you."

I stared down at the floor as everything unfolded, because the triggered image in my brain on our way to Pop's house guided me to this moment. Still, I was in complete shock to hear how she spoke to her father, whether he was correct or not. Mother grabbed our bags, and Giovanna initiated the farewell to Pop. To keep the momentum of my Mother's raging exit going, Anne and I said our farewells. Chad walked straight to the car after he grabbed most of our bags with Mother. We piled into the car as Giovanna grabbed the last few bags. When everyone was in the car, Mother screeched out of his street like she stole the car out of a dealership. We were in and out of Pop's house in thirty minutes, and on our way home.

It wasn't until we were on the parkway that I reflected on what happened in Pop's house, because the way Mother was driving scared everyone in the car. The realization that Mother had a potential pill problem shook through my bones as I replayed how Pop reacted to her medicine bag. It did confirm my suspicions about Mother making us go to the pharmacy to pick up prescription bottles on a frequent basis. What brought the muddle to light was Mother's justification to Pop for why she carried a full bag of pills, as if she would die without them. I have never seen her take a single pill from her bag to medicate herself. But then again, from a young age, Mother would come home from work and go straight to her room to sleep most of the evening and into the night.

Chad has been around for a few years at this point, and not much had changed in Mother's behavior. Whenever family members of Chad's were not at our house or there was nothing keeping her "awake," she would go straight to her bedroom. What if Mother was sleeping because of the pills, or what if she was truly sick, as she specified to Pop? I knew that Mother gave me a Benadryl whenever I could not sleep, so maybe the pills in her bag made her sleepy, too. I am certain that Mother never gave a prescription pill from that bag to any of us girls.

But why was Pop so angry? Maybe Mother was addicted to the pills and took too many. Something was not right, but I did not want to ask Giovanna or Anne for their opinion on what transpired. The rest of the car ride was silent, yet my mind raced faster than the speed of light all the way home.

A few days later, we all went to Liberty Village in Plainfield to see Chad's family members for the holidays. When Mother parked the car, I looked over to the house where the gathering looked the same as any other time that we visited Chad's family in Plainfield: a plethora of people in and out of the house, with the front door open, music blaring, and the smell of those amazing yams that his family made with the marshmallow layered on the top. I love soul food so much, and I am thankful for experiencing soul food firsthand because of Chad's family. The front door of the apartment at Liberty Village was open due to the heat coming from the oven cooking the holiday meats and side casseroles.

Nervously, I walked into the house with Anne by my side, since I knew that I could talk to her if no one else was friendly or similar in age to chat with. As soon as we walked in, we saw three girls who looked similar in age stood near the entrance to the kitchen. The youngest girl in the center of the three smiled widely. She said, "Hi, I'm Keisha, are you two twins?" She placed each of her hands on the shoulders of the other two girls and continued, "My two sisters here, Kyria and Kya, are twins, too!"

I responded excitedly, "Yes, we are twins! We are identical, are you two fraternal?" I looked at the two girls on each side of Keisha, waiting for a response, as Mother, Giovanna, and Chad walked around me to get to the kitchen and say hello to the remainder of the family.

Kyria said, "Yeah, we are fraternal, but we are still best friends." Kya nodded in agreement with her twin, and I looked at Anne as I said, "So are we, we are best friends, too. It's kind of cool being a twin, right?"

Kyria smirked, and Kya said, "Yeah, it is. Let's go eat. They are gathering the plates for us in the kitchen." Keisha said, "Nice to meet you two, and to know that I have some family my age. You guys are in what grade, seventh, like me?"

Anne responded, "Yeah, we go to North Plainfield."

Keisha's eyes lit up as she said, "Wait, we go to the same school?! That's so dope! Okay, that's even cooler! So, Chad is y'all dad?"

I said, "No, he's my mother's boyfriend, but you can say he is my stepdad. He's the only dad in our life." There was an awkward silence, because I almost explained that I just found out that Mother's friend Chris was my biological father. Instead, I smiled and unintentionally left the last statement in the air for Keisha's reaction.

Keisha patted my back and said, "Don't worry Carla, we all have our own version of where our biological dads are, and what they are doing. We all get it."

Reassured by her kind yet raw words of wisdom, I walked into the kitchen behind her and her sisters, with Anne trailing behind me. We all ate and then chatted until our departure. The visit was a good way to end the holiday break, especially connecting with others on Chad's side of the family. My desire for a connection that day literally appeared at the footsteps of the apartment door upon arrival.

With moving back to North Plainfield, Mother continued to attend the Christian church on Sundays that she became a part of while we were in Dunellen. Although I stopped singing lessons during the week at the church, Anne and I kept busy with extracurriculars in school and outside of school. Once school started up again, we joined chorus for the spring, and we returned to playing in the middle school band. It was awesome to return to our hometown at this time, because we discovered that there were even more options for sports than ever before, especially in track and field. I was also so excited to see Jayden again. It was so tough to go that long without seeing him daily. Technically, we had been together for more than a year at that point, and I yearned for our relationship to grow as we went into high school.

Alana told Anne and me about a religious Christian group called YoungLife® that her twin brothers were a part of, in which the local leaders would mentor kids and volunteer to provide free breakfast before school once a week and have events that combined fun with learning about the bible. When the kids were old enough, there was a yearly weekend trip for teenagers and local adults to gather with other YoungLife® communities throughout the Eastern Seaboard of the United States and celebrate gospel and enjoy outdoor activities, events, and games. I was ecstatic because it was an opportunity for my friends and their siblings to get together in a judgement-free zone, to hang out in a safe location, and additionally gather for the communal purpose of learning about gospel.

Alana encouraged Anne and me to wake up a little earlier than normal so we could meet Lola, a local leader at YoungLife®, and have breakfast with the group. She lived on the same street as Jayden, on Duer Street. That morning, I hoped that he would hear us walk past his house in the morning and come outside. Jayden did not come outside, so we continued to Lola's house. Alana entered Lola's house first, where we noted her twin brothers were already inside, helping her set up breakfast and organize. I smiled as I said good morning towards the kitchen, and a stunningly light-spirited, red-haired woman with an hourglass shape walked in from the kitchen area.

She said, "Hi, I'm Lola. You two look like twins. What are your names?"

Anne answered, "I'm Anne and this is Carla. Yes, we're twins. Thanks for having us here so early in the morning. Nice to meet you, Lola!"

I smiled as I observed the house, trying to understand the surroundings and familiarize myself with everything. Since Alana and her brothers were comfortable in the house and the energy felt calm, the calmness settled over my stomach.

My mind circled back to Jayden, with the desire that he would be on the doorstep to see me. As the house started to fill up with classmates like Donna, Caroline, and others, I turned around to see Jayden in my sight. He was less than a foot from me, grinning because he was going to tap my shoulder to surprise me. The energy sitting in my chest rushed in perfect distribution to my hands at lightning speed, which propelled me to open my arms to embrace him. He accepted, and whispered in my ear, "How have you been, punk? It's been too long. I missed you."

I said, "It's a long story, I can explain on our way to school." He nodded, let go of me, and proceeded to grab a plate for breakfast.

I looked past him to see Lola smiling at us. Then she exclaimed, "Oops, I forgot the pancakes on the stove!" and she rushed back to the kitchen.

As soon as Lola entered the kitchen, a young red-haired boy abruptly approached me from a side room. He said, "Hi, can you help me with my little brother Josh? He needs his diaper changed."

Jayden widened his eyes and said to me, "You know how to do that?" I glanced at Jayden and redirected my focus to the boy.

I widened my eyes and said to the young boy, "Let me see who can help me, because I have never done that before. Give me a second." I walked over to Alana where she was sitting with her brothers and asked for some help. Donna overheard and walked over to us, and we all proceeded to the side room to help with the diaper situation. Jayden stood by the doorway to observe, since he never changed a diaper either, but he was not willing to jump in and help.

Alana asked the young boy, "What is your name? You're awfully brave to watch your little brother while your mommy has some friends here."

He said, "My name is Tommy, and this is my little brother Josh."

Alana proceeded to walk me through changing his diaper, which we did together, with the help of Donna entertaining the baby.

Jayden commented in the background about how terrible Josh's poop smelled, but we got through and finished. Lola entered the side room just as the diaper change was complete. She said, "You didn't have to do that, my goodness, thank you so much for changing his diaper! I was going to do it in a few moments but thank you so much! I am so thankful. You guys are awesome!"

Jayden grabbed the plate that he left on the table, and the rest of us grabbed plates quickly to move to where the food was. We didn't eat yet, and it was almost time for school to commence. We rushed through our meal, thanked Lola for her hospitality, and walked to school. It was a good time at Lola's, especially with that feeling of togetherness that kept me uplifted.

Speaking of feeling uplifted, the energy of the Watchung house was different than the other houses we have inhabited in my gross life here. The energy was notably different in each house we moved to, in that the dark energies stemming from Forestbrook dissolved increasingly. As we made our way to unpacking items and getting situated in the new house, the bad energy was just about gone. With regards to the way that spiritual messages came through from my guides, the dreams continued in this way.

Fast Track into the Eighth Grade

Since starting school again, Jayden lived closer to me, and on weekday mornings, I made sure to wait for him front of his house until he came outside to walk to school with me. In a matter of weeks, Jayden and Kevin introduced me to other classmates who lived on Duer Street as well. Jayden and Alana introduced me to a set of twins, Julio and Julia, who lived a few doors down from Lola. There was also a boy named Cesar who lived across the street from Jayden. I became close with Julia because she laughed at my silliness and my weird sense of humor. She always told me that I was weird, but she liked it, and my presence genuinely made her happy. Their mother loved Anne and me because we were twins like her two twins, and the four of us hung out often with Alana, Caroline, Jayden, and others. Julio did not seem to care that I was dating Jayden, and he always asked me if I wanted to date him instead. I would laugh and politely decline. Our group of friends got larger as we walked home from school together, and we frequently hung out on Duer for a few hours before heading home each day.

At school, it was a few weeks until spring break of our seventh-grade year. It was time for spring sports, and I decided to join track and field with Alana and Caroline. Alana's brothers Alfred, Alvin, and Allen were already a part of the middle school and high school track and field team. Their enjoyment of the sport made us decide to try it and see if we would enjoy it, too. My twin was indecisive about joining softball or track, but she ultimately joined the track team with us.

As spring came along and we started the track and field season, the coach gave all participating students a week or so to decide which event(s) they wanted to perform at competing track events. Within days of practicing after school in the hot sun, I chose to participate in discus, shotput, and 110-meter hurdles. After the students chose events and practice commenced for the season, there were a lot of running drills and different stamina-related exercises that we were instructed to do daily.

I had a dream within weeks of the season starting that Caroline would have an asthma attack during our first track event, and an ambulance would take her away. I did not say anything in fear of Caroline becoming embarrassed. I also worried she would possibly not believe me, or that I'd cause a panic because of my dream.

As expected, we all sat on the sidelines as we watched Caroline run her first 800-meter race with a plethora of struggle. As Caroline completed the first lap around the track, she was breathing heavy and said to us, "I can't breathe, I'm having trouble. I feel like I am dying!" We watched Caroline as she slowed down as she made her way on the second lap around the track, and eventually she walked, then stopped on the track across the field midrace. Caroline remained there for a moment and put her hand on her knees as she tried to catch her breath.

I looked at Alana with my eyes widened and said, "Lala, we have to tell Coach. You think she's alright?"

Alana said, "No she's probably having an asthma attack. You know she got that purple pump thing she walks around with." She turned to her brother Alfred sitting behind us and said, "We have to tell Coach, let's get her off the track!"

Alana quickly searched in Caroline's bag to find the asthma pump and gave it to Alfred. He ran across the grass in the middle of the race and handed her the pump, and then he patiently walked to the finish line with Caroline at her desired pace.

On their walk back to the finish line, I looked over to Anne and Alana and said, "I had a dream that Caroline was going to have an asthma attack during the first race, but I did not want to freak anyone out. I feel bad because I could have done something to stop this from happening."

Alana frowned and said, "Care-bear, don't feel bad. You didn't know if the dream was real or not! This one just happened to be right. It's okay."

The messages I was receiving at this time came in the form of dreams, as I mentioned before, but one day in school the message came through directly in the middle of Italian class. It was three years to the day of Elma's death. I was stationed in the back of the classroom. It was the early morning during second period Italian class, and the thought of Elma's passing three years ago came to mind. The emotion from that day filled the bottom of my stomach and slowly made its way upward to my throat. My face tensed up as I tried hard not to shed a tear in the back of the classroom.

As I stared at my desk and the paper to refocus my emotions, images came forward in the inner window. I replayed the silence and solitude of the morning, the excitement I had for the Easter morning, and the devastating news of Elma's passing. The urge to fight my tears stopped, and I looked up to the front of the classroom. I lowered my eyebrows and looked left to right in confusion, because everyone disappeared except the teacher and one other person. The teacher was at the chalkboard, and the other person was sitting in the first chair on the row of desks adjacent to my left, looking back at me. This person sitting in the chair instantly made me forget about the other students that weren't there, because it was Elma sitting in the first chair.

She said, "Are you okay? I am checking on you. Don't worry, I am here whether or not you see me or hear me."

I looked at her, gently smiled, and recentered my focus back to the teacher. I noticed he was staring at me.

Elma said, "You're in class, so you probably should go back to paying attention." I stared at the teacher as I heard Elma make her last statement, because he was calling my name. Within seconds, the classroom changed back to the room full of students and our Italian teacher. It was magnificently different than the other experiences I had up until this time, because the room returned to its original state as I stared forward, and my eyes refocused in real time. This was not a dream in my sleep, or my third eye. This was something new that my inner window showed me, what people like to call daydreaming. That memory left me speechless, because I'd never seen with my eyes in this way. It was as if someone took a pair of glasses and layered my sight of Elma and the teacher with the original view of my classmates, but I observed it in real time.

With regards to Caroline, my friends and I went through the rest of the track season with her support on the outdoor bleachers during home games, and that was it. It was a running joke that she was "our breath of fresh air" during the home games, but she knew that we understood the severity of her asthma was serious. It was not unheard of in our group of friends for us to make fun of one another, especially if it was not harmful to the person's feelings.

During this time period, at home, Anne and I loved that Mother was busy with Chad all the time. He started to play football for a local team in Plainfield, and they would hang out with the members of the team more frequently. Whenever there were nearby football games, my twin and I would ride our bicycles to the field and sometimes attend cookouts afterward if Mother invited us. As noted earlier, Mother cooked well, but we would never come home to a cooked meal unless someone from Chad's family requested a tray of an Italian dish to be prepared. Anne and I knew basic cooking at this point, but in truth, the twenty-cent-per-container ramen noodles was our staple meal in the house.

As the school year rounded to the final stretch, Jayden and I were in a decent place in our relationship and undoubtedly content with one another. Since I got closer with his best friend Kevin, I would wait for him on the corner of my house to come outside and we'd walk to Jayden's house together. If I didn't walk with Alana, it was because she was walking with her brothers, Anne, or Caroline. No matter what, I always walked in his direction, because it was my time to spend with Jayden. When we would arrive at Duer to walk the rest of the way with Jayden, we would wait for Cesar, too, and walk with the twins once we met at the end of the street. It became a somewhat synchronized way to get to school as we made our way together each day to learn.

One morning, Jayden was taking a little longer than normal to come outside before school, and it was raining. Cesar's dad told me to come inside to wait so that we did not get wet, since I did not own an umbrella. I accepted and waited by the living room window, anticipating Jayden to exit the house. The door finally opened, and I saw Jayden putting his backpack on. Within seconds, I opened the front door of Cesar's house to walk out, and that's when I heard his father say from inside of his house, "This is not going to be the end of this conversation, I'll be damned if you are taking these kids!"

Jayden quickly closed the door again, and since he already saw us coming out of Cesar's house, I continued to make my way towards his house, since we were running a little late. Moments later, Jayden opened the door and quickly exited the house with an umbrella and his mother yelling after him, "Please cover Carla with the umbrella, she doesn't have anything on her head. Carla, where's your umbrella?"

I smiled and said, "Hi Mrs. Jackson, I forgot it at home today." In my head, I was embarrassed because I have never owned an umbrella that worked for more than two days, because they were always cheaply purchased by Mother or "borrowed" from in front of a store.

She said, "Okay Carla, well you make sure you have it with you when it's raining or snowing. Have a good day. Jayden, keep her dry." I smiled and thanked her for the advice, and we walked to school.

On the walk home from school, Jayden made sure to separate us from the group when we walked home because he knew I heard tidbits of the conversation from that morning. He said, "Look, I knew you heard a little bit of the arguing this morning from my house. My parents got into a bad argument last night after me and my little brother were supposed to be sleeping, but it carried into this morning."

I responded, "Is everything alright?"

He looked down at the sidewalk and said, "I'm not sure, to be honest. Something must have happened, because she was threatening to leave with us. I guess I will find out more as the days pass and I can talk to my mom in private."

I reassured him that maybe whatever she was upset about could be a mistake, and that they will likely be okay in a few days. I finished the conversation as we got in front of his house by gently saying, "If you need anything, I am right here. Now that I am back in town, you know where to find me. Just throw a rock at my window." I giggled, and we paused for a second. I could sense his confusion about the new situation, and I quickly kissed him goodbye before his mother came outside. I walked around the corner, where Anne, Kevin, and Alana were waiting for me to walk home.

During the summer, I did not see Jayden as much because he was playing for a traveling baseball team, and I knew that he also was traveling to Florida to see his family. I made it a point to ride by his house whenever I could, and sometimes I caught him in the morning packing up the car with his parents. If he was around for most of the day, I usually knew because Kevin would stop by and let me know he was available for us to hang out on Duer. Jayden's parents did not allow for him to venture much from his street, and I sensed that his supervision would be the norm. Meeting his parents and understanding their dynamic with their sons, Jayden and Matt, gave me the feeling of an extended family that was protective and held high standards. My family was not like his so much. Although his parents had an argument recently, I knew their support of their children was different than that of my mother.

Mother and Giovanna, on the other hand, were a part of a project that I have no idea how it came about. They were nominated to be on an episode of a television show for their weight-loss journey, on some show on NBC called *Home Delivery*. The show offered to pay for Mother and Giovanna's weight-loss surgery, gastric bypass, as a part of the show to assess the journey, but especially for her to start the schoolyear with significant weight gone. Anne and I were told about it a week or so before the show was filmed that summer. When the crew members from the show visited the house to film, they asked Mother if Anne and I could briefly speak about how excited we were for their upcoming procedure. We were both happy to see them have the procedure, truthfully, so we made a general statement to the extent of "We love our mom and sister and are glad for them to undergo the procedure."

Based on how Mother explained it to me, the gastric bypass surgery would help them lose weight. From my understanding, technically they could be healthier, which equated to happiness. If Mother and Giovanna felt happy, my logic was that the love they felt for themselves and others could potentially reflect love for their environment, which was our house. The surgeries happened fast, and the crew members came by once afterward. Mother and Giovanna were asked to go to the studio to film before and after the procedure regarding how their health was, how they felt, if there'd been weight loss, etc. The other reason this memory stuck with me was because the day that the show was filmed at the house was unexpected, in that I saw Anne do something I've never seen before.

That day, Anne and I stepped outside to the yard to get away from the cameras rolling in the house, because we were not needed anymore. I initially walked out the back door and made my way around to the front of the house to see where Anne was. Anne was on the front porch with the host of the show, Sukanya, because the crew members did not need her for filming at that moment. Sukanya was completely ignoring Anne's presence on the porch with her, as Anne did not care for her presence either. As I walked up the stairs towards Anne, Anne turned to Sukanya and asked her for a lighter, with a cigarette in her hand, ready to ignite it. I could not believe that she had a cigarette, and I widened my eyes in bewilderment that she smoked. I did not know about it until this moment.

Sukanya looked at her and firmly responded, "I did not give you that cigarette, so you better be clear to your mother if she sees you with that in your mouth."

She stared at Anne, and Anne responded, "She doesn't care, I will let her know this was all me and I have been smoking for a year. It's whatever."

I stared at my twin because I never knew, and she never told me. The feeling was a little strange to me because I believed that she would tell me everything, such as telling me that she smoked, but I didn't react externally to her and Sukanya. I smiled and stared as the silence commenced once she lit the cigarette on the porch with Sukanya.

After Giovanna and Mother's procedures, their diet consisted of easy-to-digest foods like sugar-free Jell-O and applesauce. It was much different than the Italian and soul food they were accustomed to, but it didn't stop Anne and me from eating foods after school like egg rolls and pork fried rice, pasta, and Italian subs from QuickChek® with whatever money we had. We helped Giovanna and Mother for the first week or so that they could not move around much, and we continued to support them as needed. Their weight loss was tremendous, and a wonderful thing to witness.

Anne and I also were able to meet our siblings on my biological father's side, who I will refer to as Dad onward. Dad arranged a day to come to the Watchung house and meet Chad, since he was going to be our official stepfather soon. Apparently, my mother and Chad had recently got engaged sometime that year, and they were getting married this coming summer. I did not learn about the upcoming wedding until Dad came to meet Chad. Dad came to the house, had a quick chat with Chad and Mother, and he told us that we were going for a ride to southern New Jersey to his house to meet our brothers and sisters. I sat in the front seat for the ride down and used this time to chat with Dad to learn more about him. His car smelled like Black Ice car scent, and he had a few cigars in the center console loosely displayed. I stared forward as we drove through Edison to reach the Garden State Parkway, the same way that Mother used to drive us to see Pop.

As we entered the Garden State Parkway, I asked him, "I remember what you said the other day. So, do we have more than one brother from you?"

He giggled and said, "Carla, there are a few of you running around. There are four siblings in total that you will meet tonight, but there are a few more lingering around New Jersey. These brothers and sisters you have live in the house with me."

Anne was quiet in the car most of the ride, during which she may have been analyzing Dad to understand his intentions, if any.

I smiled and said, "That's cool. I'm excited to meet new siblings, because I feel like it's just me and Anne all the time. I don't like my other siblings like that."

He stared forward but calmly responded, "Well that's okay Carla, it's understandable."

There was a long pause in between, and Dad started a new conversation by saying, "Did your Mother ever tell you guys how we met, or anything about me?"

I stared forward, and Anne responded, "No. We don't know anything, except we are here in this car with you and you are our Dad. Tell us the story on how we got here."

I looked at Anne in the back seat through the rear-view mirror with my eyes widened in judgement of how blunt she was to him. Understandably so, as we did not know Dad well and we did not know what to expect from this trip to his house or of him in general.

Dad calmly smiled in respect of Anne's tone and responded, "Well, your mother and I met because she was my teacher in my last two years of high school. She was a young thang, and I used to make her laugh so hard that she would kick me out of the classroom so she could teach. Your mother is a smart woman. Anyway, Viola and I became friends after I graduated high school and we kept in touch over the years. One night we were hanging out at a bar and got really drunk. That's when you both were conceived, and here we are. Fun fact: you were both born in the same hospital as your brother Chris, and we were all at the hospital, meaning your mother, Kenneth, me, and your stepmom, at the same time. Crazy, right? Let's just not mention that when we get to the house."

I stared forward into the oncoming highway, as he was driving ninety miles an hour. I lowered my eyebrows and said, "So wait ... my mom was your teacher?!"

He said, "Yes, that is correct, but it was her first year of teaching and she was twenty-three years old. I was sixteen. We were friends after I finished high school, because of course before then, that would have been wrong."

I nodded in agreement and remained silent the remainder of the car ride down. Anne was talking to him about basketball and other sports and music she liked.

A little past sundown, we exited on exit 102 on the parkway to go into the town of Neptune. We arrived just as my new family were finishing dinner. When Dad opened the door, two boys were in the kitchen and an older woman stared at us like a deer in headlights. Dad said, "Chris, Malcolm, meet your twin sisters Carla and Anne."

He looked at the older woman, then said, "This is my wife Rose, and Rose this is Carla and Anne."

She smiled slightly and said, "Hello."

I stared at my newfound stepmother Rose in shock, because she looked like she could pass for my mother. She was short, with the same type of hair, same skin color, and a fiery attitude like Anne. I then smiled in realization that everyone could see my face. Rose immediately instructed Dad to go with her in the other room to have a discussion. When they left the kitchen, Chris looked at us and said, "I'm pretty sure that Dad didn't tell my mom that you guys were coming. Dad never tells Mom shit." I chuckled, then frowned in response and looked to Anne as she stared around the room. She seemed emotionless to the entire situation, but I knew that she felt equally terrible that Dad did not tell his wife that we were coming. We didn't hear anything from the other room, but the four of us equally felt the awkwardness and the intense energy in the house.

Chris broke the silence and said, "You guys want to meet your sisters? They are in the living room, so we might as well get that over with, too."

Anne said, "Yeah, let's do that."

We walked into the living room, where I saw a little girl about five years younger than me, and an older woman with a newborn and a toddler boy on the floor with her. Rose and Dad walked up behind us while we stood in the doorway into the living room. Rose said, "That's Yvonne, my daughter that I had before I married your father, these are her two babies, and this is your little sister Monique."

Anne and I said in unison, "Nice to meet you both."

Everyone in the room laughed, and the conversation forward eased up in intensity little by little. No one asked about our mother or family, just general questions like hobbies, sports we played, and getting to know Anne and I only. I liked that.

Rose was very quiet, and I could feel her energy drifting through the room as us siblings hung out in the living room. Her energy filled each room she embodied throughout the evening, as if there was water boiling in a tea kettle and one can hear that whistle after the water's heated up. It was clear to me that the energy was directed towards my Dad, especially since he did not prepare her at all for this meeting of the siblings in her home. I respected that, and her, too.

There was an uncomfortable urge sifting through me, and that's when my inner window opened. The window showed me an image of Elma sitting on a folding chair with a cigarette in her mouth. She said, *"Hey, you know what to do. You need to tell her that you understand what's going on and that you'll leave whenever she pulls the white flag. Let her know, now. You're about to have your moment."*

I looked around and saw that Rose was making her way to the kitchen. My stomach was overwhelmed with emotion and humiliation, but I forced myself to slip out of the living room area and go to the kitchen where she was. My first instinct was to ask for water, and get the conversation moving this way. Feeling anxious, I nervously said, "I just want to thank you for letting us come here on a random Friday night. I did not know we would be here, and …"

She immediately cut me off and said, "It's okay, but your daddy should have let me know you two were coming so I could have cleaned the house. This house is a mess."

I smiled, and softly said, "It's okay, my house is always a mess, and we don't even have pictures on our walls. It's not homey like here. But anyway. I just wanted to tell you that if you want us to leave at any time, please tell my Dad to take us home. This is your house and I feel so bad to have walked in like this. I'm thankful that …"

She snapped back and said, "Oh no, you're okay. Don't worry about it. You don't have anything to worry about."

I stared into my cup as I sipped the water that Rose just served me, and she exited the room. Although I never experienced the level of aggression Rose exhibited versus Mother or any older woman I've ever met, I completely respected and appreciated the honest response. We equally were on the same page that the evening was unexpected and overall a shocking one, but she did not treat me like a piece of trash walking through the door. Given that Anne and I are the product of my parents' wrongdoing in their marriages, she did not take that out on us. I valued that moment, because I stood up for what was right in my heart to let Rose know that I was equally uncomfortable, yet Rose stood up for what was right in her heart to accept us into her home to meet our newfound siblings.

Dad drove us home that evening, and it was almost midnight by the time we arrived. Anne did not say much about the evening as we settled down in our bedroom. She was quiet and seemed unfazed to have met new family members. When I settled into bed, Anne told me that she had to leave, and she would see me later. She asked me to keep the window open so I could hear her and open the door later. When she left into the night, I turned off the bedroom light to act like I was going to sleep. I peeped out of the window to see what she was up to. She went into the garage, grabbed a backpack, and hopped on her bike. She rode away. Anne's random venture into the night was the first time I had seen her leave like that and not return until five in the morning. I remember her walking in the house and saying, "What?" when I would wake up and look at the alarm clock, noting that it was practically morning. I could tell she was firm in her prerogative of not letting me know where she was, and I left it at that. Whatever Anne was up to, I knew that she did not want me involved.

A few days after we met our paternal siblings, Caroline's mother and Mother agreed that Caroline could stay at our house for a month during the summer and spend time with us. It was convenient because instead of Grandma driving her to my house every day and trying to coordinate with her own schedule, she just left Caroline with us for the month. We had so much fun hanging out throughout the day. We walked to Plainfield to go shopping on Front Street for our school clothes, hopped on the train to go shopping in Newark, rode bicycles to the West End of town to see Keisha and friends, and played manhunt with other friends between our town and Dunellen, and often visited the arcade in Dunellen. We took advantage of every waking moment. We usually planned our days in advance, so we felt like we were on a vacation schedule, and on the days that we wanted to do activities that were too far for a bicycle, Caroline's grandma happily drove us. We planned with Grandma to go see a movie at the theater in Mountainside, go to Short Hills mall to walk around, or go roller-skating at Skate 22 whenever the funds were available to us. Skating was one of my favorite things to do with Anne and Alana, even though Caroline was not so good at it. She would lose confidence when she was skating decently and do a stage-like dramatic fall while pulling whoever was next to her. It was honestly one of the most entertaining things to witness Caroline do, she was so terrible at it. She thought it was funny, too, but she really sucked at skating.

Caroline was an important part of our lives because she kept Anne, Alana, and me in the right perspective of how to treat others who are doing right by you. A lot of times we were frustrated with Caroline because of how she would speak to Grandma and her mother, as if they were expected to bring us anywhere if we made the plans for them. If there were last-minute changes in Grandma's schedule and she couldn't drive us, the three of us would not be bothered—if anything, we were thankful to have had the opportunity to get driven. We knew that our mothers wouldn't drive us around, because Alana's mother had to work as a single mom for her five children. Our mother, as we know, was too busy living in a fairytale of depression with Chad. We were not appreciative of how Caroline treated Grandma, and we often called her out on it. We were patient with her when we spoke to her about it, because we did not want her to feel attacked by our friendly advice. In short, we urged Caroline to be thankful for a ride from Grandma, since us three did not have an opportunity even as simple as that, most of the time.

Caroline's visit did not alter how Anne and I went about our day, but at night we switched around how we slept since we had the two twin beds from our younger years pushed together into one. It formed a synthetic full bed. It was difficult for the three of us to fit there, especially since Anne and I tossed a lot in our sleep to begin with. We took turns sleeping on the floor after a few days of trying to fit in the bed, because it was simply too hot to sleep. Our room did not have an air conditioner, and there was no central air, but thankfully Eric installed a window fan for the summer.

After two weeks of having Caroline sleep over, we started to have evenings when Caroline and I would not be able to sleep, and we would talk while Anne snored loudly over the sound of the window fan. Some nights Anne went out with her infamous backpack and bicycle, but other times she would leave earlier in the day and be gone until midnight. On one night, Anne left per usual and it was just Caroline and me. We could not sleep, so we talked about things we went through in our life thus far as we snacked on some chips in the bedroom. It was getting later into the night, and Anne finally came home around three in the morning. Anne giggled with us for a few minutes as we deliriously explained that we were waiting for her arrival, and she let us know that she needed to get some rest. She got onto the bed and immediately fell into a deep sleep. It was as if she ran a marathon or biked miles and miles, because she seemed exhausted. She started snoring loud, and we looked at each other in anticipation for the long night ahead. Caroline said, "Well, I hope we can fall asleep now, because we are tired, but Anne is snoring so loud."

I said, "Yeah. But we should be okay." I took out the king-size sheet set that I borrowed from the hallway closet and laid the flat sheet on the floor to serve as our bed. Anne had already sprawled out on the bed, and the snoring was so loud.

Caroline and I got under the fitted sheet as she said, "Do you think that Anne has a girlfriend or something, or maybe she's selling something out of that backpack, like marijuana?"

I turned to her and said, "I don't know what marijuana is, but I don't know, to be honest. Anne has not officially told me she likes girls, even though we both know, but I am not going to push her to say anything she's not ready to."

Caroline said, "Speaking of girlfriends, how are things with you and Jayden?"

I said, "Good, I guess. I don't get to see him much and I am shy around him because I do not know if I am moving too slow or fast for him, or if his parents think I am not good for him. I don't know. That new kid Darrell has been around more, and I think I may date him for a little instead."

She responded, "I get you. What do you mean by moving too fast, or too slow?"

I said, "You know how Alana is dating that guy, Ronnie, and Darrell is best friends with him? I sometimes see them when I am not with you, because Alana brought me with her to see Ronnie. They are always tongue kissing and stuff, so I feel slow in doing things because I haven't done that with Jayden yet. Maybe Jayden thinks I am moving too slow since we have been together for a year and a half now. I don't know."

She paused for a moment to process what I said, then asked, "So wait, you haven't tongue kissed Jayden yet?"

I said, "No. I want to, but I don't know how to do it. I'm nervous that I'll do a bad job, then he will break up with me or something. You know how boys are—they expect females to be like a black stallion running through the meadows, as if we know how to do everything and be seductive for them."

She laughed and said, "Yeah. Boys will be boys."

I nodded in agreement and slightly frowned at the thought of it.

Caroline said, "So, do you want to learn how to? I mean, my friend Lexi and I taught each other because it is not easy. I don't mind showing you. Is that weird? I mean you're like my best friend, so I don't want you to think it's anything more. Just want to help you, girl, and look out for you when the time comes."

I widened my eyes in confusion, and nervously said, "Ah, yeah. Sure. I know what you mean. Umm, so how would we do this? You would explain it to me, or?"

She giggled and said, "No, silly. I would have to kiss you to show you and do it until you can kiss correctly. You have to go in a motion sort of like in movies, like this …"

She grabbed my face and started to make out with me. It felt so strange for two milliseconds, because she was my best friend, but more than anything, because I did not ever think I would kiss a girl. As she was physically teaching me how to tongue kiss, my mind raced into different emotions, such as how strange it was to be kissing someone the same sex as me. It made me wonder if Caroline liked girls ever since her first experience of tongue kissing with her friend Lexi. I wondered if this meant that Caroline may like me, too.

Caroline paused and proceeded to straddle on top of me, and she continued to make out with me. The kissing moved into our clothes coming off, and her taking the lead, since I had no idea what I was doing. For a split-second I thought about how Lexi and she must have gotten this far, too, to having sex with Caroline, but my mind went back to how intense the night became. We were together on our bedroom floor as I shared my first sexual experience with a female, which was beautifully spontaneous. I was dumbfounded as everything unfolded while Anne continued to snore nearby, because I did not feel pressured to be in this moment with Caroline. On the other hand, I absolutely loved what was happening. My first sexual experience felt safe, with my best friend, and immediately changed my perspective on only liking boys. Even though I never had sex with Jayden, since I was in middle school and expectedly a virgin due to the age, I knew from this experience with Caroline that there was more that I desired from my love life. From that day onward, I hoped for one day to date a girl to have the full experience.

Caroline and I did not date after this moment but remained best friends. However, I needed to tell Jayden what I did behind closed doors. It did not feel right in my spirit to let this go without mention. Thankfully, Jayden had minimal to no reaction, and he said, "That's okay with me, if you are not kissing other boys, then I don't care. So, you like girls now too, huh?"

I stared at him in amazement that he legitimately did not care that I had sex with Caroline, and I responded, "Yeah, I guess I do. It was actually supposed to be a practice make-out session, for you, and it turned into that." I giggled because of how silly I sounded, but it was the truth.

He grinned and said, "Wow Carla, just wow. Well, you must have done a good job practicing. Now is it my turn, you know, since I'm your actual boyfriend?"

I said, "Of course." We experienced our first tongue kiss, and walked to our favorite restaurant within walking distance, La Strada. From that day forward, I knew that I could tell Jayden everything and anything because of how calmly he would react to my actions.

The Eighth Grade

The first day of school was different in terms of esthetics. When I "picked up" Jayden on the way to school, I noticed that the Acme supermarket was knocked down and there was a CVS Pharmacy being built to replace it. Although this meant the students had the CVS for snacks and stuff after school, I was not pleased to see the grocery store disappearing. This meant that if I needed food, I would need to buy food from local restaurants instead of buying food to cook. The nearest grocery store was off Route 22, about a ten-minute drive from my house. My twin and I could not make it on foot or bikes even if we tried.

Once school started to roll into motion, Jayden and I were inseparable and stronger than ever. When our birthdays in October and two-year anniversary arrived later that month, we were at an all-time high of love and true friendship. I opened my heart to him about the situation with my parents who never dated a day in their life and cheated on their marriages to have us twins; about Kenneth and Elma's deaths; about what my brother had done. I went into depth about my gift of receiving information ahead of time in many different forms and the communication with my guides; and where my mind was wandering outside of our growing relationship. My happiness with Jayden had nothing to do with how my spirit felt collectively, in which my spirit was sad and conflicted with wounds that he could not fathom. This was the time when the pieces started to come together in my life, during which I began to realize that my life was deeply abnormal. I did not have supportive parents, older siblings to look up to, meals prepared for me at home or any sort of schedule, and us twins had each other to lean on for everything: to make sure we ate at least once a day and had the toiletries to style our hair, brush our teeth, and wash the dirt from our gross bodies.

At Jayden's house, his parents' fighting continued, so much that his mother would leave for days at a time. His parents never recovered from the initial incident of what I have assumed to be infidelity a few months prior, and they were not shy about bickering in front of Jayden and me. His parents knew that Jayden and I had dated for two years, and they recently let me come into the house to hang in the living room. Given that the living room was decorated by dolphins of all shapes and sizes, which spiritually represents harmony and being instinctual, their house energy was intense in the timeframe that I was there. The energy felt newly altered, and Elma reminded me every time I walked in the house. Elma always mentioned that the energy in Jayden's house was not always like that.

On another note, Caroline and I continued to have sex a few times after that day, and thankfully our friendship remained separate of the fling we carried onward. Although we did not decide to be girlfriend and girlfriend ultimately, we still enjoyed each other's company whenever no one was around. It was something that became a part of our routine, and we never told Alana or Anne since we were not ready to.

Around the wintertime, however, Anne officially sat me down to let me know that she liked girls and had no interest in boys. She reminded me of how weird it was to hold Jayden's hand years ago, and that she briefly dated one of Alana's brothers, but things did not feel right in that relationship, either. She asked me not to say anything, because she was not ready for the entire world to know. Anne explained that she told Mother already, and as Chad nodded in the background she replied, "Okay, I already knew that you were gay, so thanks for letting me know. Good thing you won't get pregnant. That's one less child that I have to worry about."

Mother's reaction did not surprise me, because she did not care, as I expected. A few days later, I was walking through the hallways with Alana when I saw Anne standing around with the middle school and high school girls from the basketball teams, as well as some other sports jocks in the school. The urge to tell Alana about the recent news about Anne skyrocketed through my bones, and I leaned over.

I whispered in Alana's ear that Anne just officially told me that she was gay, and she completely lost it.

She screeched, "What? Anne is gay?!"

Anne turned and looked at me, and instantly walked away from the area in complete embarrassment. As she walked past, her eyes flooded with tears of frustration. She did not say a word to Alana or me, and I stared at Alana.

I said, "Why the fuck would you yell that, Alana, what the fuck is wrong with you! I whispered for a reason. Oh my God ..." Alana's eyes were completely widened in disbelief, because she did not know what to do. The damage was already done, and everyone heard.

We closed our lockers and walked around the bend in the direction of where Anne was headed, especially since we noticed the basketball team girls standing near Anne moments before had followed her direction. As we made our way to the end of the hallway, we heard yelling and arguing. When we turned the corner, that's when we saw several girls punching and kicking Anne to the floor, and her fighting them all back as best as she could. There were more than six girls putting their hands on her and yelling nasty comments about her being gay.

We jumped in, attempting to break things up, but a few teachers and other students already started to pull the girls off my twin. I asked Anne if she was okay, and she told me to go fuck off. I went through the remainder of the school day with constant thoughts about what transpired, and I was so livid at Alana for reacting the way she did. I knew by that point that anything I told Alana could go public, depending on how she reacted.

Anne was sent home during the school day because of her injuries, and Mother came home early to be with her in support.

When I arrived home, Giovanna was waiting for me in the dining room with a chair in front of her, and Mother met me at the front door. Anne was upstairs, and Mother said to me, "So, you're the one that told the whole school about Anne being gay, when she could have easily done it herself when she was ready to? How dare you embarrass your twin sister like that. Go have a seat in that chair in front of Giovanna. *SUBITO!*"

I attempted to respond, and Mother slapped me across the face as hard as she could. She told me that I was a disgrace to the family and now I was going to pay for it. In tears, I slowly walked to the dining room, where Giovanna was waiting for me. She had a pair of scissors in her hands, and a handful of twine. My chest instantly tightened up, and the anxiety instantly filled my body. I knew what she was going to do. Mother forcibly sat me in the chair as Giovanna tied my hands behind my back with a piece of twine and tied my chest around the chair with a belt.

When I was completely secured to the chair, Mother said, "Since you love your hair so fucking much, Giovanna is going to give you a shabby haircut so you can feel the embarrassment as long as Anne will for what happened today. Payback is a bitch."

Giovanna held the top of my head still and began to butcher my hair. My hair was straightened that day, which in hindsight benefitted me because my hair is naturally unruly and curly. Giovanna happily cut my hair four to five inches and continued to cut more as she went around the base of my head. She sculpted a mushroom cut on my head as shabbily as she could.

I stared forward in disbelief of what was happening, and I felt like my spirit was stripped from me. It was a wake-up moment for me, because I could not believe Mother would do something this gruesome to one of her children. Mother had put her hands on us on several occasions, but in my eyes, that was normal. This was a scarring punishment, which in hindsight was only the beginning of more to come from her. As I stared forward with tears rolling down my face in silence, Anne came to the bottom of the stairs and stared at me. I looked in her direction and she had her mouth open in disbelief. She turned and walked upstairs. I guess she didn't know that was coming.

When Giovanna finished her haircut, she left me tied there for three hours until I begged to pee. Mother untied me. Mother then went to her bedroom to grab her instant camera, and she told me to stand there as she took photos of me. She passed one of the photos to me and told me, "It's for your memories. Enjoy it."

When everyone went to bed, I left into the night for a walk. I wore a black hoodie and black clothing in case I needed to hide from the police patrolling the town, and I walked for hours around town reflecting on my life. I felt the lowest I have felt in my life thus far, like a complete disgrace.

I went to school the next day and didn't pick up Jayden on the way. I walked by myself and fought my tears, because I knew my face would be puffy and red if I cried. As I arrived at school, Alana and Caroline both yelled, "Oh my God, what happened?!" and everyone looked over to me.

Jayden arrived and said, "Babe what happened to your hair? I waited for you, but are you okay? Who did this to you?!"

I ignored him, put my head down and walked to the school bathroom until the bell rang. I did not want to be seen. I cried on and off for the entire school day. The school counselor called me into his office and wanted to talk to me about what happened to my hair. I declined talking to anyone and morbidly went through the next few weeks in school in silence.

My spirit felt defeated, and my mind spiraled around how I could get away from this dysfunctional family. After this incident, we saw Eric at some point and he initially laughed for a few seconds when he saw my hair but immediately felt bad about it. He got us a Boost mobile phone with the walkie-talkie to share between Anne and I so that we had someone to talk to. We were both having a rough time, but in different ways. The phone benefitted Anne and me because we discovered that Dad had one, and my little brother Chris also had one. When one of us would leave the house, that person would take the phone with them. There were multiple days of silence between Anne and I, and her evenings out in the streets increased significantly. It was as if we were having a breakup and did not want to be around one other.

During this time of sadness and dark thoughts racing through me much of the time, I did not disclose as much to Jayden or my friends because I did not want to burden them with my strong feelings of not wanting to be alive anymore. The nightly walks or runs at the track in the middle of the night helped a little, but I focused on writing poetry to try to soothe my sadness over my life in whole. I started with a composition notebook that I "borrowed" from school and filled each page with poetic emotions from Chris's wrongdoings, living in a household that did not want anything to do with us twins, the mystery behind Mother's pills and constant dormancy in her bedroom since I was five years of age, and the loss of Kenneth and Elma. Maybe life could have been better with one of them in this gross world with us, but they stuck around to guide me spiritually when needed. For that, I am thankful that the triggers sent from my guides have brought me to this state of realization that there was work to be done. The work to be done was within me, but also within my household.

In school, I continued to play the clarinet in band and sang in chorus. They were my only positive channels for enjoying life at the time. As the spring commenced, I participated in track and field again. That year, I broke the record for discus-throwing for middle schoolers. I guess that may have been due to the emotions firing in me, because the throwing came simply for me. Middle school graduation was approaching, and the fighting between Jayden's parents did not let up. On the other side of things, Giovanna reminded us that Chad and Mother would be getting married sometime in the summer. It was a whirlwind of news to hear that they would be getting married and we needed to buy a dress for the wedding. The wedding would occur in our backyard at the Watchung house, which I will cover in the next book.

The springtime of the school year went very fast and a lot happened in the period of a few months. My dreams continued to come forward vividly with information about me, Jayden, Caroline, and Mother. One dream involved me walking to an area of town to meet with Caroline, and we were talking on the phone while looking at one another a block away. As she was walking towards me in the dream, a car came screeching down the road and hit her on the corner of the street where she was crossing, pinning her body to the concrete street sign. The dream felt immensely real, but I did not tell anyone about it. It seemed too irrational to speak on.

A few weeks went by and there I was, meeting up with Caroline on a Saturday morning and talking to her on Mother's Nokia phone that she let me borrow for a few hours. I was chatting with her as I walked past the Bagelmasters shop on Somerset Street, and turned the corner of Howard Street to where the bank was. Caroline was two blocks up on Howard, coming towards me.

She said, "I see you! I can't wait for us to get this shopping over with, I just want to find our graduation dresses already!"

I smiled, and before I could respond the inner window came forward. My eyes widened as the dream replayed itself, with her body pinned on the concrete street sign, more rapidly than I dreamt. I looked at her walking towards me and I calmly said, "Caroline, I need you to walk a little faster to me. You know what, I want you to run to me. NOW!"

She said, "Oh my God, Carla, what did you see? You're scaring me. Why do I need to run, is something behind me?"

She looked back and did not see anything, then said, "Carla, you're scaring me."

I responded, "Please, Caroline. Just do me a favor and run towards me right now. I'll explain when you get over here, but I need you to stop talking to me and run." Caroline had on a pair of Chinese mesh slippers that were popular in the 2000s, which made me giggle when I saw her take them off before running as fast as she could towards me in fear. I giggled, but I was nervous. I did not know if this car was truly going to crash on the street moments later as it did in my dream.

I watched Caroline cross the street as she yelled, "Carla, I'm scared!" her voice full of anxiety, and I saw her take a few more steps towards me. Then, the expected happened, as in my predetermination: a car came screeching down the road and hit the concrete street sign on the corner.

Caroline, on the other hand, was still running towards me and not pinned between the car and the sign. She looked back to see the car crash, mid-morning on the corner, and she began to cry. I was in complete shock because I was not sure if this was going to happen, but rather, I was trying to ensure that Caroline was safe. I hugged Caroline with grace in my heart and tears flowing with joy because she was okay. We looked back to see others from the bank and houses nearby rushing to the scene of the accident, and we hurriedly turned the corner and started our errands to find the graduation dress for us.

As we walked down Somerset Street towards the clothing stores in Plainfield, I told her more about the spiritual experiences that I hadn't told her already, with much more detail. She was all open ears as I explained that it was strange and unexplainable, but I did not fight it. Caroline and I told Alana and Anne what happened later that day, and we asked them not to tell anyone because I was still in shock of how accurate my dream was. Whenever another friend like Sammie, Julia, Keisha, Donna, or Alana's brothers would hear me explain something spiritual happening to me, their facial expressions gestured to me that I was misunderstood. I tried to avoid these conversations around other friends whenever possible, and sometimes will not bring up that I am spiritually gifted to this day.

Although I had a spiritual gift that I did not understand, I was thankful that the triggers were the guides.

Jayden and I were preparing for his parents' separation and divorce because they notified us in the springtime of their marital status. His mother was moving out of the house by the end of the school year, and she was not going to take Jayden and his little brother with her.

Around April, whenever I was not in school or track, Elma constantly came to mind. I was missing her presence on this gross Earth. Every time I brushed my short hair that was barely growing or heard one of her favorite songs, my mind wandered into sadness. I was trying to be supportive of Jayden and the changes happening in his house, but I was so emotionally broken.

Jayden called me over to his house sometime in May, after I dropped my backpack off at my house. He had something to tell me. When I left the house to walk over, Kevin came up from his house behind me, to walk with me. When I made it to the corner of Dupont and Duer Street, I turned the corner to see Cesar outside with Jayden. They were all in the street, waiting for me.

I looked to my left and right, then I said, "Why am I here, are you breaking up with me or something?"

He paused, took a step closer, and said, "I need to tell you something. No, we are not breaking up." He stepped closer to me, put his hands on my shoulder, then whispered, "I am moving away next month. I am so sorry, I just found out. We all wanted to be here to support you when I told you the news."

I pushed him away in anger and feelings of neglect from his end. He was leaving me in this town, but forever. How could he expect this relationship to work? I responded, "No. This can't be real. Why would you do this to me?" I reacted by pushing him again, and again, and again as tears built in my eyes.

Still facing me, Jayden started to back away from me down the street towards the front of his house. I took my shoe off and threw it at him. Kevin grabbed my arms from behind and told me to calm down. He said softly, "Carla, you know it's because his parents are splitting up. You can't let this bring you down. There's nothing we can do."

I stared at Jayden as Kevin hugged me and made sure that I didn't break away from him.

Cesar said, "Well, that's all folks," and he left for his house.

After I calmed down, Kevin let me go and walked to the corner to give Jayden and me some space. I cried in anger, and with feelings of brokenness all over again.

Jayden said, "Look, let's talk more in the morning tomorrow, okay? We can make this work, because I still want to be with you." He kissed me on the forehead, hugged me, and walked into his house.

Kevin waited for me, and we walked home together. Kevin listened to me vent about how depressed I have been overall and how happy Jayden made me feel. He offered his ear to me and thanked me for opening up to him. I hugged him and went back to my house. I cried for the rest of the evening.

THE EIGHTH GRADE

The next few weeks were my last with Jayden living three blocks away, graduation of the eighth grade, Mother and Chad preparing for their wedding, and hopefully nothing else catastrophic to add to the next few strange weeks of life.

Mother's life was circling in my visions through dreams, in that soon she would let us know something she'd been holding back from telling us for a long time. The information that she had been holding back for a long time was that her father, Pop, was not her actual father. Her father had been in the witness protection program for years now, but in this moment before her marriage with Chad, she wanted to start the ongoing quest to find him.

In the beginning of this book, I mentioned that my maternal grandfather's whereabouts were discovered recently, but this was the first time that I heard about Mother going in search of her biological father. Her mind was constantly focused on other things, and not so much on more important matters like her children. During this time, I dreamed of Mother hiding something from me when I walked into her bedroom, and her keeping the things in her room a secret. Mother was the mystery that I wanted to understand, but more so, I wanted to understand why she did not love us the way we wanted to love her. There was something deeper than what I could see with my eyes about how outlandish her behavior had been. One day, I would learn more about her.

As the remaining days approached for graduation, Anne and I found matching blue dresses with Mother because she insisted that the dress purchased for graduation would be the same as the ones for her wedding. Mother told us that we did not need to have two dresses for the separate events because it was a waste of money.

Two days before our middle school graduation ceremony, Anne and I were outside playing manhunt with friends until late evening. We arrived home at around ten in the evening to see Mother, Chad, Eric, and Giovanna sitting around the living room area, talking amongst one another with someone that I never thought I'd see again. My older brother Chris was here from the military early for dishonorable discharge, and he was catching up with everyone but us in the living room. He also had a female with him, apparently his new girlfriend named Sarah.

Anne and I stared into the living room in complete surprise and sadness to see Chris permanently home in the living room. My heart sank to the floor as Mother stated, "Surprise, your brother is home! He will be sleeping upstairs in the attic since all of the bedrooms are full."

I nodded and looked around the room to see everyone unfazed that he was home, sitting by Eric. Chris said, "Hello, Carla and Anne. You both seem to have developed a lot. You two look beautiful."

Eric looked at me with the acknowledgement of my mixed feelings about his arrival. I looked around in disbelief that no one made a comment of Chris's instant inappropriateness about my growing body. I ignored Chris and walked up the stairs without saying hello in return. With everything I felt in my spirit from Jayden's family moving, depression, and dealing with my recently bumpy relationship with Anne, Chris's arrival was an absolute shock to me. There was no way to determine how my life would turn in the next few months into high school and onward, but I was unquestionably concerned about my mental state. I was now older and could fight him off if I needed to, but he was over six feet tall. I knew that it was me against the world in this household.

Graduation was so much fun with my classmates, but afterward on my walk home in my dress and heels, I felt gloomy. I knew that my summer would turn into a whirlwind of emotions as I transitioned into high school. There was a lot to process with the recent changes in my household and life. Jayden was set to leave two days after graduation, and he made sure to call my Mother's cell phone and ask for me. Jayden asked me to come by so he could say goodbye, but I only had ten minutes to arrive before he got in his father's car to drive to his new home in Mount Olive.

I jumped on my bicycle and rode as fast as I could to see him, but I hit a crater on Coddington and skidded a few feet on my knee. My right knee had a huge gash in it, but I got back on my bicycle and continued to pedal forward to his house. As I rode to his house to say my final goodbye, the thought of how strong my spirit was to keep on my path to my destination, to see Jayden one last time, reminded me of who I have been all along. I was a powerhouse, and I could conquer through anything life handed me. The ride to Jayden's house represented my life at the time, with the pain stemming from the open wound on my knee and blood gushing down my leg onto my sock. No matter the circumstances, I made it to my destination before it was too late. I made it through the window of time I was allotted despite the struggle on my way. When

I arrived at Jayden's, I gave him the longest hug I could give him before his father told him to get in the car, and I sat on my bike with tears filling my eyes as I watched him get into his father's car. I watched happiness drive away.

Epilogue

The next steps in my ongoing journey will be covered in the sequel to this book, *Triggers are the Guides, Part II*. In the next book, the journey continues through my teenage years and the intensifying moments that lead me to the first feelings of adulthood and freedom.

Be sure to look for *Triggers are the Guides Part II,* scheduled for release in 2022, for an action-packed read through the toughest years to come. It will unravel several layers in my journey which I fought through in pursuit of an open door.

Acknowledgements

I would like to first thank my editor Marie Valentine for her intricate review and feedback in my manuscript, and my cover design artist Toushai for creating a powerful way to present the novel in one beautiful image.

I also would like to thank my friends, and family for their support from childhood until today. There's so many to name, but you all know who you are. Each person in my life, from friends to family, has given me something as I have given them. I would not be half the person I am today without those who have been in and out of my life through the years. This work of creative nonfiction is for all your support, love, truth, and hurt.

To my husband, thank you for your protective love of my heart, my spirit, and patience in everyday activities as I created this manuscript. This world is tough, and I'm grateful to have met you along the way.

To my coworkers, in-laws, friends, and spiritual colleagues, thank you for cheering me on through the writing process, through life, and keeping me sane when I felt discouraged to power through the manuscript. You were instrumental in motivating me to finish something on my bucket list.

This manuscript is for you all. Thank you all for the impact you have had on my life thus far.

Summary of the Clairs

Before I continue, I would like to briefly go through the significance of the Clair senses that are mentioned a few times throughout the book, as well as what it means when I mention the "third eye." The below is a brief description of each of the Clair senses, concrete enough to understand why the triggers are the guides, and not just for me, but for you, too. Whether you, the reader, understand or believe the above exists, energy does not lie. One could call them vibes, gut feelings, intuition, daydreams, or vivid dreams, but in the end, the energy does not lie.

Triggers can be your senses in many ways, as the senses can be described as physical, subconscious, or spiritual. As we know, there are five main senses related to the gross body. In addition to the gross body, there is the subtle body, which encompasses several separate energy components of what many refer to as the soul in conjunction with the spirit. Your subtle body brings life and power to the function of the senses, organs, the mind, and thoughts. It is composed of many sheaths (layers around your body in the form of aura-like energies) of an individual, relating the gross body to the mind, energy, and discernment. There are many sheaths in subtle energy, which identify as the seven interfacing auric bodies projecting from each individual.

For example, have you ever attended an event such as a wedding and immediately stopped whatever you were doing to look at the person entering the room because you felt their presence? That is a perfect example of someone entering the room and expanding their subtle body and other sheaths of energy while entering a space. How about when you thought about a friend that you have not spoken to in years and suddenly, you receive a message or phone call from him/her? This example demonstrates that your outer subtle body was already in contact with the subtle body of the friend, which led to their hunch to contact you.

The subtle body in tandem with the gross body will register informational downloads in the different forms of what people like to familiarize as a "sixth sense." The brain, as expected, also demonstrates activity when this occurs. In the umbrella of possibilities through the sixth sense, our intuition registers this information using "Clairs." The word Clair means *clear*, derived from the French language that goes as far back as the Vikings era. The Clairs consist of senses like our physical five senses that we learn about early on. However, the Clairs exist through the subtle body with the assistance of the gross body. The commonly recognized Clairs are defined as follows:

- ❖ Clairvoyance, clear seeing through visions of extrasensory visions/images. This is the "third eye" and "inner window" that I speak of in the book.
- ❖ Clairaudience is the clear hearing via thoughts and/or information obtained by extrasensory communication

(higher self, spirits such as loved ones, sometimes an unknown spirit).

❖ Clairsentience, clear feeling of emotions or physical feelings of others, noticing energies. Empaths usually identify with this Clair before the others and often feel drained in crowded settings, or after being around people.

❖ Claircognizance, clear knowing and divine receiving of information. Common for "left-brained" people, but it is the intuitive ability to have drop-in insight immediately. A good example is knowing information without being taught.

❖ Clairalience, clear smelling of smells on an extrasensory plane. For example, walking into a room with a group of friends, one person recognizes the smell of something distinct like vanilla, but no one else smells it. *Your grandma liked vanilla, and that was for you.*

❖ Clairgustance, clear tasting on an extrasensory plane. An example would be having a taste in your mouth when communicating with someone (physically or psychically).

References

Map of North Plainfield, New Jersey. Created by hand.

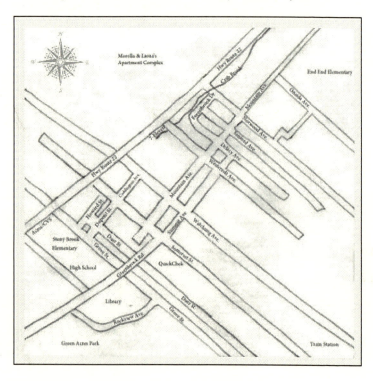

Psychic Mediumship

1. Katz DL. *You are Psychic.* Woodbury, MN. Llewellyn Books. 2013.

2. Nohavec J. *Where Two Worlds Meet: How to Develop Evidential Mediumship.* San Diego, CA. Aventine Press. 2010.

3. Winkowski MA. *When Ghosts Speak: Understanding the World of Earthbound Spirits.* New York, NY. Hachette Book Group. 2009.

Cell & Gene Therapy

American Society of Gene & Cell Therapy. Different approaches. Available at: https://www.asgct.org/education/different-approaches. Last accessed Oct 2020.

Sickle Cell Trait

Naik RP, Haywood Jr C. Sickle Cell Trait Diagnosis: clinical and social implications. *Hematology Am Soc Hematol Educ Program.* 2015 December 5; 2015(1): 160-167.

Multiple Hit Theory

Dash S, Kinney NA, Varghese RT, Garner HR, Feng W, Anandakrishnan R. Differentiating between cancer and normal tissue samples using multi-hit combinations of genetic mutations. *Nature Scientific Reports.* (2019) 9:1005 | DOI:10.1038/s41598-018-37835-6.

Made in the USA
Middletown, DE
07 March 2021